MW01680627

THE BRITISH TRADITION I

Poetry, Prose, & Drama from the Old English & Medieval Periods (449-1485 A.D.)

Student Guide

David M. Wright

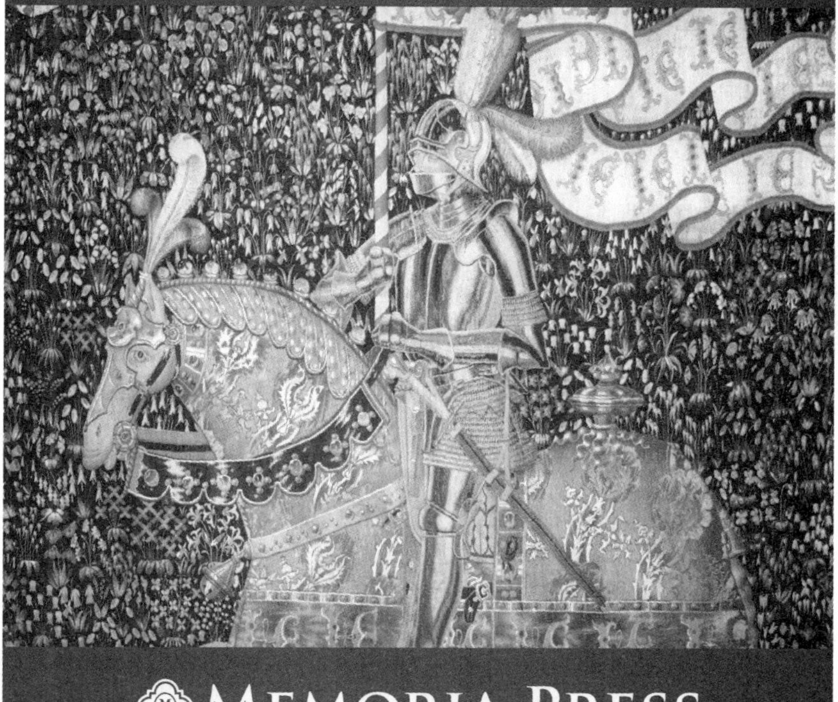

MEMORIA PRESS

MEMORIA PRESS
www.MemoriaPress.com

THE BRITISH TRADITION I
Poetry, Prose, & Drama from the Old English & Medieval Periods (449-1485 A.D.)

STUDENT GUIDE
David M. Wright

ISBN 978-1-61538-992-6

Second Edition © 2017 Memoria Press | 1122

All rights reserved. No part of this book may be reproduced in any form
by any means without written permission from the publisher.

Contents

How to Use This Study Guide with the Text & Literature Notebook

A Step-By-Step Plan

INTRODUCTION AND PREPARATION

A. First read through the Notes & Instructions to Student (pp. 6-7).

B. Read the two introductory essays, "Taking With Us What Matters" and "Four Stages to the Central One Idea" (pp. 11-19).

C. Read "How to Mark a Book" (pp. 20-21).

D. Open *The British Tradition I: Poetry, Prose, & Drama from the Old English & Medieval Periods (449-1485 A.D.)* and read the Introduction "Warrior & Priest," marking the text in key places according to the method taught in "How to Mark a Book."

E. Complete the Comprehension Questions over the Introduction (pp. 24-26).

BEGIN TEXT PROPER

1. Begin with the Pre-Grammar section (p. 27). This prepares the mind, at least in some small way, for the reading and study of the poem and, ideally, for the Central One Idea.
2. Read through the Reading Notes closely, stopping occasionally to discuss or clarify.
3. Next, try to define as many words from the Words to Be Defined section as possible in your Literature Notebook. For meanings of words that you cannot figure out from the context given, consult a dictionary (or refer to the word in the text for more context) to help you choose the correct definition from the Definitions Bank. This vocabulary work will help you better understand and comprehend the text as you read.
4. Now, read thoroughly and well the particular poem delineated by the Study Guide (e.g., "Elegy Written in a Country Churchyard"), marking the text in key places according to the method taught in "How to Mark a Book."

5. Return to your Literature Notebook and finish defining any remaining Words to Be Defined. If need be, refer to the word in the text for contextual help, or in a dictionary, of course.
6. Answer the Comprehension Questions in your Literature Notebook, stopping to discuss and referring to the text when necessary.
7. Discuss and reflect upon the Socratic Discussion Questions, referring to the text often or when necessary. These are intended for verbal discussion, and they also provide a good opportunity for you to take notes in your Literature Notebook. The teacher may also assign the questions to be answered in written form in your Literature Notebook.
8. Complete the Rhetoric | Expression—Central One Idea section. Take the time to consider and reflect upon the Central One Idea; discuss freely, making room for disagreement as well as convergence.
9. Complete the Writing Option in your Literature Notebook at your teacher's discretion.
10. Repeat steps 1-9 for each section.

Notes & Instructions to Student

- This Study Guide is intended to be used with *The British Tradition I: Poetry, Prose, & Drama from the Old English & Medieval Periods (449-1485 A.D.),* published by Memoria Press.
- This Study Guide is best used in conjunction with a good-quality notebook, which will henceforth be called the **Literature Notebook**. You will be expected to complete most of the activities in your Literature Notebook. And of course, the Literature Notebook will be the place for all of your notes during reading and discussion, and for all of your essays.
- Though I recommend that, ideally, you complete the entire Study Guide in conjunction with reading and discussing the text—I also recommend that you **adapt the Study Guide to your particular context**. This means you should feel comfortable using the Study Guide in a way that best suits the needs of your teacher and your class—in a manner that fits your schedule, number of meetings per week, time allowed for discussion, and total time for the unit, etc. This could mean that your teacher may have you complete fewer vocabulary words and questions, etc. This is fine, and I encourage it. I have written the Study Guide comprehensively to provide a maximum number of notes, words, and questions—so that you will have plenty of work to complete, rather than wishing there was more.
- This Study Guide is written in such a way that it can be used for grades 8-12. If you are in grades 8 or 9, additional guidance, assistance, and adaptation will probably be helpful.
- Pages 24-26 in the Study Guide feature comprehension questions over the introductory essay "Warrior & Priest" (449-1066) in the text. Another set of comprehension questions are included in the Study Guide over the introductory essay "Knight, Priest, & Commoner," for the second section of the text (1066-1485). These comprehension questions are useful for you to complete, but they can also be completed orally in class discussion, in groups, or in another manner that suits your teacher's judgment.
- Poems are cited by line number (l. 23), or stanza and line number (4.2).

- You will notice that many questions ask you to quote a line(s) from the text in your answer. This will help develop your ability to find evidence in the text to support your answer. It will also develop the skill of synthesizing quoted material into your written argument, which is an important skill for analytical essay writing.
- The Reading Notes section contains some helpful notes and facts along with some of the difficult words and phrases in each poem.
- The Words to Be Defined section contains *specific* words chosen because they are both *challenging* and *useful* for you to learn and memorize.
- Some of the essay prompts tend toward a shorter essay, and some toward a longer. Both short essays (1 page or less) and long essays (2-4 pages) are useful and helpful, depending on the intent and purpose. Your teacher will convey his or her expectations regarding the length of the essay.
- In the Comprehension and Socratic Discussion Questions, I sometimes use the words "paraphrase," "summarize," or "provide a brief summary." All of these essentially mean the same thing.
- The *Everyman* section of the Study Guide thoroughly covers four key sections of the play, but the entire play is included in the anthology. Thus, your teacher has the option to have you read only the four parts of the play that are covered in the Study Guide (an abridged reading), or the entire play. My suggestion is that you read the entire play, but this will depend on how much time and focus your teacher wishes to spend on *Everyman*.
- A Rhetoric Essay Template is provided in the back of the Study Guide as another pre-writing option to help you outline your essay before you undertake to write it. The template is very similar to the Rhetoric | Expression section. Your teacher may choose to have you complete the Rhetoric | Expression section or use the guide.
- As a kind of "final achievement" that celebrates the reading of the text and completion of the Study Guide, complete the Memorization & Recitation section at the end of the Study Guide. Perhaps more importantly, this section allows you to move on from the poems with a special part of them in your heart.

Basic Features & Background

1. **Anglo-Saxon lyrics** - Anglo-Saxon lyrics were composed primarily for simple memorization and recitation.
2. **lyric poem** - a poem that expresses the thoughts and feelings of a single speaker
3. **elegy** - a sustained, formal poem that mourns the loss of someone or something; a lament or sadly meditative poem on a solemn theme
4. **Anglo-Saxon lyrics contain these elements**:
   - **regular rhythms** in the lines, often with strong beats
   - **kennings** - A kenning is a two-word metaphoric word or phrase that takes the place of a noun. Example: "whale-road" for *sea;* "swan-boat" for *ship*.
   - **alliteration** - the repetition of consonant sounds in successive words
   - **assonance** - the repetition of vowel sounds in successive words
   - **caesuras** - The poetic device in Anglo-Saxon poetry that divides each line in the center into two half lines (more noticeable in the original Anglo-Saxon than in many modern English translations). Example: "Night after night || over the misty moor" (*Beowulf*)
5. **diction** - the particular words used in a work; word choice
6. **shift** - a major change in structure, tone, or subject in a poem or novel
7. **personification** - a figure of speech that gives human qualities to animals, inanimate objects, or ideas
8. **anaphora** - the repetition of a word or words at the beginning of two or more lines, phrases, or clauses
9. **apostrophe** - a figure of speech in which someone (usually absent), an abstract quality, or a non-existent personage is addressed as though present
10. **rhyming couplet** - two lines in a poem, usually equal in length, with end words that rhyme

11. **scansion** – the scanning of a line of poetry to mark its stresses and meter
12. **enjambment** – in poetry, the continuation of a sentence without pause beyond the end of a line, couplet, or stanza
13. **dream vision** (or dream allegory) **poem** – A type of narrative poem that was especially popular in medieval literature. In a dream vision poem, the poet pictures himself falling asleep and envisioning in his dream a series of allegorical events or people. The dream vision device allowed for the more fantastical world of personifications and objects of symbolic nature characteristic of medieval allegory.
14. **allegory** – a form of extended metaphor in which objects and persons in a narrative, either in prose or verse, are equated with meanings that lie outside the narrative
15. **Morality Plays** – *Everyman* is a morality play. The genre developed during the medieval period in Europe and featured allegorical dramas with characters who personify moral qualities or actions, such as Good-Deeds and Confession; or abstractions, such as Beauty and Death. Their purpose was didactic, that is, to teach moral lessons. Scholars date *Everyman* around the year 1485.
16. **prosopopoeia** – A figure of speech in which an imaginary, absent, or deceased person is represented as speaking.
17. **epigraph** – A motto, phrase, or quotation set at the beginning of a literary work (or one of its divisions) to suggest a theme.
18. **epithet** – An adjective or brief phrase used to characterize a person, place, or thing, summarizing its most essential quality. For example, in the *Everyman* play, Everyman, speaking about God in lines 595-597, uses a number of epithets: "O *ransomer* and *redeemer / Of all the world, hope and conductor / Mirror of joy*, and *founder of mercy*."
19. **ballad** (also known as the folk ballad or traditional ballad) – A song, transmitted orally, that tells a story.
20. **suspense** – Anxiety created by the writer to make the reader wonder what will happen next.

21. **rising action** – The part of a plot which complicates the action. It begins with the exciting force, gains in interest and power as the opposing individual(s) or forces come into conflict, and proceeds to the climax, or turning point.
22. **climax** – The moment of highest and greatest tension in the story.
23. **conclusion** (also called resolution or dénouement) – "The untying of the knot"; the conclusion or resolution that follows the climax.

Taking With Us What Matters

The Transformative Power of Reading for the Central One Idea

David M. Wright

Sometimes our study of literature resembles a kind of clinical laboratory lesson. We encircle the text in our white coats ready to dissect the story (or poem) like a dead animal. Or if this sounds too invasive or scientific, then we *analyze* the text in order to extract the "elements of literature" (the title of a recent bigpress high school English textbook)—to know the work by studying its parts. Or perhaps we analyze simply to have a meaningful artistic engagement with the text.

All of these, though, fall short of what our true purpose and intent should be when reading a Great Work. But ironically, this very purpose may be the most overlooked. This brings to mind a few similar yet related aphorisms: What we go about searching everywhere for is often right in front of us or within us; overstimulate the senses, and they sense less; keep it simple; less is more.

What we are missing in our modern study of literature is a conscious effort to uncover the soul of the work, the *essence* from which it derives its being—a fundamental, ontological reality that I have named the *Central One Idea.* Searching for and determining the Central One Idea profoundly shapes our interaction with the work and the trajectory of our study. There are seven reasons why this is so.

First, by doing so, we honor the work. Just as we notice an innate hierarchy in the natural world, in societies, organizations, and families, we insist that a kind of hierarchy exists in the work as well: there is one idea at the heart of the story; one idea burning as the sun in its solar system, with many planets (literary elements) in rotation around it. This idea gives the work its ultimate meaning and its greatest expression. In this idea, the other elements find their raison d'être.

Second, I often ask my students, "What's in a title?" to which they reply, "Everything." Then I ask, "What's in a name?" and they promptly reply, "Everything." I repeatedly ask this not only because repetition is the mother of learning, but also because I do not want them to miss what is right in front of them: The title of a work often hints at, points toward, or outright expresses the Central One Idea.

Why parents think deeply about the name they give their child reiterates this point. Names matter; they represent the potential character and nature of the child. In this spirit, I chose the name Central One Idea carefully so that its nature and purpose would be inherent. It does not roll too quickly off the tongue, but instead demands a certain level of consciousness to express. It is *central*; it is *one*; and it is an *idea*. In other words, it is central to the work and stands above other ideas, determined then to be subideas; it is singular; and it is a complete idea, that is, a proposition with a subject and a predicate, not just a subject.

Third, when we consider the essay, the academic paper, the dissertation, or any other nonfiction work, we insist that it must have a *thesis*. The thesis is everything to that particular work—so much so that, ontologically, the work derives its being from its thesis. It is no mystery why many high school and college English teachers demand that their students underline the thesis in their papers—to combat their students' shoddy understanding of what a thesis is and why it is so important.

In the nonfiction genre especially, the title almost always encapsulates the thesis. Take, for example, the academic bestseller some years ago: *Guns, Germs, and Steel: The Fates of Human Societies*. Here Jared Diamond argues that the varied developments of human societies on different continents are the result of environmental determinism—geography, population, and agriculture—and more specifically, that Eurasian technological and economic rise and dominance stemmed from their superior weapons (guns), their diseases which weakened indigenous populations (germs), and their centralized government which fostered powerful military organizations (steel). One can almost read the title, absorb the thesis, and devote 500 pages to something else, say Hugo's *Les Misérables*.

Is a novel, play, or poem really any different than a work of nonfiction? Does not fiction express a thesis just as nonfiction? I believe it does. If not explicitly, then implicitly—for it must express *something,* and that *something* is the Central One Idea. As well, that essential idea is that which *compels* the author to put pen to paper, or the artist to put brush to canvas. The novel, poem, or painting is simply (and profoundly) the artistic medium or rendering of the idea.

So what, then, does a Central One Idea look like? In Charles Dickens' *Hard Times,* the owner of a school instructs his students in "nothing but facts" and finally realizes that his program ruins the humanity of his students. The Central One Idea: Life should be lived with imagination rather than by an overemphasis on logic and cold facts. In Herman Melville's *Billy Budd,* a young sailor is falsely accused of mutiny. The Central One Idea: Human nature is both pure and corrupt, just as physical nature is both beautiful and harsh. (Yes, these could be said in various ways; and yes, others could be argued for, but I'll get to this in point six.)

Fourth, reading for the Central One Idea moves our methodology back toward the classical and medieval, toward what C. S. Lewis called "the discarded image." In previous ages, the *idea* and *truth* had a kind of unity and primacy that is lost in modernity. I think here of Plato and his forms, Aristotle and his organized classification of reality, Dante and his fixed and ordered cosmology. The moderns prefer fragmentation, subjectivism, and deconstruction of both the idea and truth. More comfortable with truth shattered into shards, this age insists that reality is broken and disconnected, not whole and unified.

Approaching a work of literature with this broken and distant framework means students are uncomfortable asserting any one truth about a story—too afraid to insist: *This is the fundamental idea that drives this novel.* They are more satisfied pointing out elements in the work that stand out to them rather than ascribing primacy to any one; or more often, they prefer expressing *how the novel makes them feel.* As well, they might focus undue attention on a character they like or dislike based on whether the character behaves in a way acceptable to contemporary (politically correct) standards.

Fifth, the Central One Idea might be the primary factor in the movement from novel to *Great Book.* It is difficult to find any Great

Book without a prominent Central One Idea. The book becomes timeless and great for two reasons—one, it has an important Central One Idea; and two, because that idea is expressed with masterful artistry, form, and beauty.

Sixth, determining the Central One Idea engenders logical thought and rhetorical speech. It demands close reading and analysis, supporting evidence and proof; it generates critical discussion and rhetorical writing. The nous (in patristic thought, the eye of the heart) of a work is not always easy to find. Sometimes it is everywhere present but cannot be directly seen. Sometimes it has to be wrestled for in the midst of competing ideas. Sometimes it seems too obvious and simple. But nonetheless, teaching the work in this method requires the student to stake a claim for one central idea. The student must then defend his or her Central One Idea with evidence from the text, the Study Guide, scholarly sources, or his/her own logic. And this stimulates fruitful class discussion and debate, and leads directly to the essay and composition.

Finally, reading for the Central One Idea is the essential way to study literature because it is an act of discovery. Since we desire by nature to know, we experience joy when we discover new things and complete gaps in logical sequences. We seek so that we may find. The joy of learning comes from the Elysian fount of discovery. May we let our search for and insistence upon the Central One Idea become the *logos* of our study of the Great Works, and find there wisdom and virtue.

Four Stages to the Central One Idea

Using the Trivium to Uncover the Heart of a Work

David M. Wright

UNDERSTANDING THE SEQUENCE AND STAGES OF THE STUDY GUIDE

Because discovering and internalizing the Central One Idea in a Great Work is vital for a proper reading and for cultivating wisdom and virtue, it necessitates that the Study Guide embody this conceptual framework. Thus, the guide is written in such a way as to lead the student (and teacher) through four stages to the acquisition and expression of the Central One Idea.

The four-stage sequence is rooted in the trivium—grammar, logic, and rhetoric—which has vestiges from the order and way of learning spanning several ages since antiquity. In the trivium, grammar is language; logic (dialectic) is thought; and rhetoric is expression. Put another way, in the grammar stage, one accumulates the fundamental elements, features, and facts of a body of knowledge. In the logic stage, one arranges, connects, organizes, compares, and reasons with the facts learned and draws a conclusion(s). In the rhetoric stage, one expresses that conclusion/truth to others.

Sister Miriam Joseph defined the trivium as the three arts of language pertaining to the mind: grammar is the art of inventing and combining symbols; logic is the art of thinking; and rhetoric is the art of communication.[1] She also states it in this way: grammar is concerned with the thing-as-it-is-symbolized; logic is concerned with the thing-as-it-is-known; and rhetoric is concerned with the thing-as-it-is-communicated.[2]

The trivium, she says, is the organon, or instrument, of all education at all levels because the arts of grammar, logic, and rhetoric govern the means of communication—namely reading, writing, speaking, and listening. She adds, "Because

[1] Sister Miriam Joseph. *The Trivium: The Liberal Arts of Logic, Grammar, and Rhetoric.* Ed. by Marguerite McGlinn. (Philadelphia: Paul Dry Books, 2002) 3.

[2] Ibid., 9.

communication involves the simultaneous exercise of logic, grammar, and rhetoric, these three arts are the fundamental arts of education, of teaching, and of being taught. Accordingly, they must be practiced simultaneously by the teacher and pupil."[3]

As well, the trivium is a movement from distinct parts into synthesized whole. The three stages guide the student to relate the facts learned into a unified, organic whole. This encompasses the aim and purpose of this guide—to move from elements and parts toward the unity and wholeness of the Central One Idea.

Marguerite McGlinn, introducing Joseph's work, says, "The trivium teaches us that language evolves from the very nature of being human. ... We invent symbols to express the range of practical, theoretical, and poetical experiences that make up our existence. ... Words are characterized by their relationship to being and to each other. When a speaker or writer uses a word, thus assigning it a particular meaning, it becomes a term and enters the realm of logic. ... The linguistic symbol is then translated into a logical entity ready to take its place in a proposition."[4]

We can see, then, that the trivium has much to do with being human, with negotiating our lives. It has an ontological reality within us through our use of reason and language. The four-stage sequence developed for these Study Guides is trivium-based because the trivium embodies how we think, how we learn, and how we communicate.

In our particular context of studying a Great Work, the teacher has firmly in mind the abstract singular truth that he or she wishes the student to learn, which is the Central One Idea of the work. Several other salient ideas inherent in the work will be discovered and learned along the way, but it is the Central One Idea that is the ultimate aim and purpose of the study. Knowing the destination is vitally important in this four-stage sequence. Though popular culture may be fond of saying, "It's not the destination that counts, but the journey"—nothing should be

---

[3] Ibid., 6-7.

[4] Ibid., viii.

further from classical teaching and learning. Both the journey and the destination count, but especially the destination, which is the understanding and expression of the idea.

THE FOUR STAGES PROCEED AS FOLLOWS:

Stage 1: Pre-Grammar | Preparation

To begin, the Pre-Grammar stage prepares the student for receiving and understanding the Central One Idea by invoking his prior knowledge, experience, or interests concerning that idea. Just as Socrates believed that the truth he wanted his interlocutor to understand was already within him, in some way or part, the Central One Idea is already the soil within the student. Thus, it is helpful to cultivate the soil in preparation for planting the seed. In this preparatory stage, the student is merely asked a few questions about something related to the Central One Idea, or simply about the basic plot or subject of the work—to set him thinking in a certain direction. The Study Guide features two or three questions that aim to do this, but may be supplemented with different questions or with discussion as the teacher sees fit. This is the shortest stage and can take as little as five minutes (though fine if longer).

Stage 2: Grammar | Presentation

In the Grammar stage, the student is presented with and discovers essential facts, elements, and features of the story (or play, poem, etc.). Here the student encounters many useful facts in the Reading Notes and learns new vocabulary words in the Words to Be Defined section. In addition, the student becomes grounded in the basic features of the story through the Comprehension Questions and learns new literary and rhetorical terms (that appear in bold throughout both the Grammar and Logic sections). In this stage, the student is presented with the basic grammatical units—facts, elements, features, ideas—that comprise the work. She begins to familiarize her mind with new subject matter. New *types* or *particulars* are presented and discovered here.

Stage 3: Logic | Dialectic

In the Logic stage, the student *reasons* with the facts, elements, and features of the story/poem; sorts arranges, compares, and connects ideas—and begins to uncover and determine the Central One Idea. He *compares* the new ideas and facts with similar things already in the mind, which gives rise to new conclusions. Importantly, the final conclusion, the Central One Idea, is often an *abstract* or *general* truth, though it may be expressed by means of a story's particulars, such as a character's action and discovery, etc. The best method for leading the student toward this new abstract truth is through the Socratic method. Hence, this stage features Socratic Discussion Questions, which are different than the Comprehension Questions in the previous stage because they go further up and further in to abstract thought. Simply put, they are deeper questions with the intent of leading the student toward the Central One Idea. The Socratic Discussion Questions are intended for verbal discussion, and they also provide a good opportunity for the student to develop his note-taking skills in the Literature Notebook. The teacher may also assign the questions to be answered in written form in the Literature Notebook.

At the end of this stage, the student should be ready to make a determination of what he thinks is the Central One Idea. This is not always easy, but the student should be encouraged to take this step, a kind of "leap of faith"—though not a huge leap over a dark chasm, but a short step relying on logic and evidence from close reading, work in the Study Guide, notes in his Literature Notebook, and attentive perception and reflection.

It should be noted here that this general truth may now be exemplified in new cases and applied to new circumstances, one of which will be the expression and defense of the Central One Idea in the Rhetoric stage.

Stage 4: Rhetoric | Expression

In the final stage, the student expresses what she believes to be the Central One Idea. The student's ability to organize and express her thoughts in the Literature Notebook is an important skill in the Rhetoric/Expression stage, though the essay template in the Study Guide works well, too.

In this section, the first question asks the student to briefly summarize the plot, and the second question asks the student to express the Central One Idea in a complete sentence. The reason for this is so the student will be forced to distinguish between a plot summary and the Central One Idea. The two are quite different. The former, of course, concerns the sequence of events in the story. The latter concerns a larger *abstract* truth—the central proposition at the heart of the story.

The third question asks the student to list three supporting points for her determination of the Central One Idea. The fourth and fifth ask for the opening lead and the closing amplification. Finally, the student should choose and copy down a Central Quote as well as write the teacher's version of the Central One Idea—which is helpful for several reasons, the first of which is that it enables the student to draw a comparison.

In the last section of the Rhetoric stage, the student is presented with the opportunity to write an essay—to express her Central One Idea, the thesis she must argue for and defend in her essay. This improves the student's writing skills and increases her rhetorical abilities. Options for other essays and writing activities are also presented.

How to Mark a Book

1. Underline all important passages.
2. Place a vertical line in the margin next to very important passages which you have already underlined.
3. Place an asterisk next to key passages which you have already underlined and which already have a vertical line in the margin next to them.
4. Make notes in the margin to indicate important points made in the text.

Example:

Reading is a conversation

Mortimer Adler points out in *How to Read a Book* that reading is a conversation between the reader and the author. You read a book, presumably, in order to learn from the author, but this process is not just a passive process on your part. The reader understands, questions, and sometimes must argue with the author. The highest respect you can pay an author is to respond—positively or negatively—to him. The markings in a book are an expression of that.

There are several devices that can be used in marking a book or article. Each has a different purpose.

Underline

First, you should underline important or forceful parts of the reading. This will normally be done on about 15 percent of the text. However, no more than 30 or 40 percent of text, even in a very key reading, should be underlined.

Use vertical lines

Second, you should use vertical lines in the outside margin to emphasize text that you have already underlined. Normally, no more than about 10 to 25 percent of the text you underlined in any reading should be marked in this way.

Use asterisks

*

Third, you should mark any text that stands out as one of the one to three most important statements in the book, chapter, or article. This will be text you have already marked with a vertical line in the margin. Mark it again, using a star, asterisk, or other doodad. If the passage is truly extraordinary, you can mark it with two of these markings. If it is life-changing, you might even try three, but you should find one of these very seldom.

Write notes (or numbers) in the margin.

Fourth, you should make notes and write numbers in the margin. Making notes can reduce a complicated part of the text to a simple statement or record a question that a passage raises in your mind. Numbers can also be used to record a sequence of major points or to indicate where else in the book the author makes the same points.

You can also put a double line for any text that is not only important, but quotable or aptly stated.

From the ANGLO-SAXON INVASION to the NORMAN CONQUEST

449-1066 A.D.

Introduction

Read the Introduction "Warrior & Priest" in* The British Tradition I*, marking the text as you read, according to the method taught in "How to Mark a Book."

COMPREHENSION QUESTIONS

1. ________, in the course of his conquest of ________, crossed the English channel in ____B.C. The inhabitants of the island at this time were ____.
2. A century later, ____led a campaign that established the Roman rule in Britain in ____ A.D. The inhabitants of the island at this time were ____.
3. The Romans had little difficulty colonizing Britain northward into Scotland. List four activities/accomplishments that they introduced in the process of colonization.
4. Why were the Roman legions withdrawn from Britain?
5. Which people eventually submerged the remnants of the Roman Empire in Britain and built what would become the English nation? Where did they come from?
6. Identify the two social classes of these tribesmen, and provide a brief description of each class.
7. Warriors from these two classes owed a deep and sacred loyalty to their ____ in a time of war. In a time of peace, this leader was a wise judge and a generous bestower of ____ to the warriors for their services.
8. What were the important necessities for each member of the tribe?
9. In the fourth and fifth centuries, who came pouring into Europe, not to be checked until they had penetrated into France?
10. What three Germanic groups felt the pressure from these invaders and were consequently forced to migrate westward across the North Sea?

11. As the story goes, why did Vortigern, the king of the Britons, invite and welcome some of these restless wanderers to his island?

12. Thereafter, the ____ steadily nibbled away at the Eastern British coastline, setting up temporary and permanent settlements, until the whole region was in the hands of the Germanic invaders.

13. The process was slow, but the end was inevitable. By the middle of the____, the ____ held England in their possession.

14. Who was the greatest of the West Saxon kings, and for what did he have to fight for his very life?

15. What was significant about England when King Edgar died in 975?

16. After King Edgar's death, there were more Danish invasions, political wranglings, and partisan strife. Then what significant event takes us out of the Old English period into the beginning of the Middle English period?

17. What were women primarily valuable for in these Germanic warrior tribes?

18. What was the warrior's code?

19. What new individual was to subtly change the life of England, to smooth off the rough edges of the warrior's personality, and to bring him to a totally different world—the world of knowledge and culture?

20. Though the seeds of Christianity had been sown in England during the later years of the Roman occupation, and kept alive through missionaries from Ireland and St. Patrick, the great flow of Christianity into England came straight from ____, when in the year ____, ____.

21. The coming of the priests meant, first of all, a new religion in England, of a ____which was wholly opposed to the ____.

22. The Anglo-Saxons, like all their Germanic fellow-men, worshiped the ____: ____, ____, ____, and others, who were divinities of heroic mold, but also projections of the tribesman's own ideals and perceptions of ____.

23. Christianity brought several fields of knowledge to the Anglo-Saxon. List four.

24. Define "epic tradition."

25. The ____ of a hero were a source of inspiration to members of the tribe; and the belief in a hero was ____.

26. What was the business of the bard, or minstrel? And what did the Anglo-Saxons call him?

27. Such is the origin of the ____.

28. What is the one full-length epic surviving in Old English?

29. The prevailing lyric note in Old English poetry is the ____ —impersonal thoughts on the ____, melancholy and often undeniably poetic.

30. Since all recorded Old English literature dates from Christian times in England, the process (of Christian influence) was inevitable. Why?

31. Old English poets Caedmon and Cynewulf are considered ____, ____and their product is what we call ____.

32. Who was the most heroic historical figure in the Old English period? What was he the presiding genius of?

33. But (in Old English literature) there is a fierce idealism as well: a conception of ____, and of ____, a stern fidelity of ____ that lives again and again in the battle poetry.

34. In the end, it is apparent that the Viking Anglo-Saxon has achieved at least the forms and disciplines, and possibly the spirit, of ____, incongruous as the blend of ____and ____may be.

35. In that fierce and grinding ____ (____), the Old English civilization sank in honorable defeat. ____, ruling all England with a stern and effective hand "by the splendor of God," stood as the harbinger of a new, more varied age.

THE LITERATURE OF THE WARRIOR

The Seafarer

PRE-GRAMMAR | Preparation

Prepare to think about the poem and its Central One Idea by drawing upon your prior knowledge, experience, or interests.

1. Imagine living life on a ship at sea, away from your family, friends, and community. Now imagine you are in this place of exile permanently. How would you feel? What things and people would you yearn for? What kinds of dreams and hopes would sustain you?
2. How would the vast ocean make you think or feel about life, eternity, and God? How would it shape your perspective about these realities?

GRAMMAR | Presentation

Discover essential facts, elements, and features of the poem through the Reading Notes, Words to Be Defined, and Comprehension Questions.

READING NOTES

1. **Anglo-Saxon lyrics** – Anglo-Saxon lyrics were composed primarily for simple memorization and recitation.
2. **lyric poem** – a poem that expresses the thoughts and feelings of a single speaker
3. **elegy** – a sustained, formal poem that mourns the loss of someone or something; a lament or sadly meditative poem on a solemn theme

4. **Anglo-Saxon lyrics contain these elements**:
   - **regular rhythms** in the lines, often with strong beats
   - **kennings** – A kenning is a two-word metaphoric word or phrase that takes the place of a noun. Example: "whale-road" for *sea;* "swan-boat" for *ship.*
   - **alliteration** – the repetition of consonant sounds in successive words
   - **assonance** – the repetition of vowel sounds in successive words
   - **caesuras** – The poetic device in Anglo-Saxon poetry that divides each line in the center into two half lines (more noticeable in the original Anglo-Saxon than in many modern English translations). Example: "Night after night ‖ over the misty moor" (*Beowulf*)
5. **diction** – the particular words used in a work; word choice
6. **personification** – a figure of speech that gives human qualities to animals, inanimate objects, or ideas
7. **anaphora** – the repetition of a word or words at the beginning of two or more lines, phrases, or clauses
8. **oft** (l. 2) – often
9. **benumbed** (l. 5) – made numb, especially by the cold
10. **prow** (l. 6) – the bow; the front of a ship
11. **gannet** (l. 15) – a large seabird with mostly white plumage
12. **kittiwake** (l. 15) – a small gull that nests in colonies on sea cliffs; its loud call sounds like "kittiwake"
13. **sea-mew** (l. 16) – a common seagull
14. **tern** (l. 17) – a seabird related to the gulls, somewhat smaller and more slender
15. **pinions** (l. 19) – the wings of a bird
16. **aught** (l. 37) – anything at all
17. **yore** (l. 64) – in the past; long ago
18. **sear** (l. 68) – dried up; withered

WORDS TO BE DEFINED

Definitions Bank

assigned; committed

complaining; grumbling; fretful

dwelling places; residences

great waves or surges of water

someone or something that indicates what is to come; a forerunner

stormy; turbulent

has a strong inner feeling or notion that something bad will happen; foretells or predicts

to praise enthusiastically; to exalt

to pull, twist, or turn forcibly

trivial; unimportant

1. 'Mid the terrible rolling of waves, **habitations** of sorrow. (l. 4)
2. Yet hotly were wailing the **querulous** sighs round my heart (l. 8)
3. Some hardship, some **trifling** adversity, proud and wine-flushed. (l. 22)
4. To test the the high streams, the salt waves in **tumultuous** play. (l. 27)
5. Nor in aught save the roll of the **billows**; but always a longing (l. 37)
6. Summer's **harbinger** sings, and forebodes to the heart bitter sorrow. (l. 44)
7. Summer's harbinger sings, and **forebodes** to the heart bitter sorrow. (l. 44)
8. **Wrench** the soul away, doomed to depart. This is praise from the living (l. 56)
9. 'Gainst the malice of fiends, and the devil; so men shall **extol** him (l. 59)
10. He has seen his old friends, sons of princes, **consigned** to the earth. (l. 71)

Read "The Seafarer," marking the text in key places according to the method taught in "How to Mark a Book."

COMPREHENSION QUESTIONS

1. When was "The Seafarer" probably composed?
2. "The Seafarer" reminds us that the Anglo-Saxons were originally ____, and their daily lives were vitally connected with the____.
3. This poem, along with passages from "The Wanderer" and voyages in *Beowulf*, is the beginning in England of a ____.
4. Who is the **speaker** in the poem?
5. In the opening five lines, how does the speaker describe his voyages? List five **descriptive words** or phrases that he uses to describe his voyages.
6. Quote the line that contains an instance of **personification** in lines 8-11.
7. Consider the **diction** in line 11. What particular word signals a broader **theme** for the poem?
8. What important **contrast** does the speaker present in lines 10-11?
9. In lines 11-13, what evidence do you find that the seafarer's pain is more than physical?
10. What elements of **setting** does the seafarer mention to help convey his desolate, exiled state? Quote at least three words or phrases.
11. What **transition word** signals the first important **shift** in the speaker's perspective about the sea? Quote the line or two that contains the shift, and underline the transition word.
12. What change does this **shift** bring in the speaker's perspective? Quote a line that you think best expresses his change in perspective.
13. What kinds of things does the seafarer choose to live without in favor of the "roll of the billows"?
14. Identify two **kennings** from anywhere between line 22 and the end of Part I. The kennings in this translation may have more than two words.
15. Part II presents another major **shift** in the poem. What do you think has caused the seafarer's changed perspective?

16. What three things make life so uncertain and "wrench the soul away"?

17. In the first ten lines of Part II, the seafarer is primarily concerned with:

- **a.** the angels
- **b.** the earth and its pleasures
- **c.** the afterlife
- **d.** violence, age, and disease
- **e.** enduring hardships

18. Quote the line that contains the use of **anaphora**.

19. The seafarer presents another **shift** in the last section of the poem. Where does his attention or focus now turn? Include a line or a phrase from this section in your answer.

LOGIC | Dialectic

Reason with the facts, elements, and features of the poem; sort, arrange, compare, and connect ideas – and begin to uncover and determine the Central One Idea.

SOCRATIC DISCUSSION QUESTIONS

May be verbally discussed or answered in written form in your Literature Notebook.

1. What sounds of society does the seafarer imagine hearing, and what sounds does he actually hear? How does this **contrast** contribute to the overall **mood**?

2. Quote the 2-3 lines where the seafarer reiterates and **amplifies** the **contrast** between a city-dweller and himself. What important words or expressions does he use to convey how he feels about those people?

3. *But that he has always a longing, a sea-faring passion*
For what the Lord God shall bestow, be it honor or death. (ll. 33-34)

These lines bring together the desire for the sea and the will of God. **Summarize** and explain these lines. What important idea is conveyed?

4. How does the seafarer describe nature in lines 39ff.? Include a line or phrase from his **description** in your answer. What effect does this nature have on the seafarer?

5. Read lines 72-74. **Summarize** these lines. In your answer, identify and explain the **metaphor**. What is the main topic the seafarer is speaking of?
6. In the last section of the poem, the seafarer is concerned with not only the object of our belief, but in how we should ____.

RHETORIC | Expression

Express in your own words the Central One Idea with supporting points.

RHETORICAL EXPRESSION

To be answered in your Literature Notebook in preparation for your essay.

1. In 2-3 sentences, **summarize** the poem.
2. Write the **Central One Idea** of the poem in a precise, eloquent sentence.
3. List two or three points that **support** your determination of the Central One Idea.

◈ **Central Quote:** *Choose a line or two from anywhere in the poem that you think best embodies the Central One Idea. With good penmanship, write it in your Literature Notebook.*

❶ **Write the Central One Idea as expressed by the teacher.**

WRITING OPTION

Can people find a manner of life or a place in life where they are fully happy? Or, like the seafarer, will they always have a yearning for another place? Are we all, figuratively speaking, "seafarers"? Develop a clear thesis that presents your point of view and support it with a well-reasoned argument. Though most of the essay will be your own ideas and supporting evidence, make some effort to reference "The Seafarer" in your essay. For example, you may find that the seafarer and/or his story work well as an analogy or metaphor in your argument, or in a certain part of your argument. You may find it useful to quote a line from the poem in your essay—one time or even a few times.

The Wanderer

PRE-GRAMMAR | Preparation

Prepare to think about the poem and its Central One Idea by drawing upon your prior knowledge, experience, or interests.

1. Imagine that you are a warrior or bard (singing poet) of an Anglo-Saxon clan. Now imagine losing your entire clan in a war. You are now wandering alone on the English countryside. What are you thinking about? How do you feel? Where are you going? What are you going to do? Describe your thoughts and feelings.

GRAMMAR | Presentation

Discover essential facts, elements, and features of the poem through the Reading Notes, Words to Be Defined, and Comprehension Questions.

READING NOTES

1. **scops** - Traveling storytellers (bards, minstrels) who memorized and passed along an oral tradition of stories and songs, usually celebrating the deeds of a hero. Some of these stories were eventually written down.
2. **Exeter Book** - An early anthology of manuscripts comprised of selections from this bardic tradition. It was most likely compiled by monks during the reign of Alfred the Great in the later decades of the ninth century. The survival and discovery of the book is a fortuitous wonder. The book has several stains from a drinking mug, a large burn, and cut-like marks that suggest it may have been used as a cutting board! Without this book, many stories from this bardic oral tradition would have been lost. Famous Anglo-Saxon lyrics such as "The Seafarer," "The Wanderer," and "The Wife's Lament" were all discovered in this collection.
3. **rhyming couplet** - two lines in a poem, usually equal in length, with end words that rhyme

4. **apostrophe** – a figure of speech in which someone (usually absent), an abstract quality, or a non-existent personage is addressed as though present
5. **ruth** (l. 1) – pity or compassion
6. **sooth** (l. 2) – truth
7. **fain** (l. 8) – eager; compelled
8. **mead-hall** (l. 22) – The social hall central to the Anglo-Saxon tribe's community and social life; the place where the lord, warriors, and tribe would celebrate important events such as a victory over another tribe in a war, and where bards (minstrels) would sing about the heroes of their tribe and their tribe's history.
9. **fere** (l. 24) – companion
10. **rime** (l. 36) – frost
11. **vaunt** (l. 55) – boast
12. **weal** (l. 58) – wealth; well-being
13. **lorn** (l. 68) – lonely and abandoned; forlorn
14. **byrnied** (l. 74) – dressed in a coat of chain-mail armor
15. **Wyrd** (l. 80) – fate; personal destiny

WORDS TO BE DEFINED

Definitions Bank

a profoundly wise man	merriment; amusement
brave and persistent	mixed; blended
chains; restricts	pale; weak
deprived of or lacking	presented; conferred
showing care and thought for the future	to feel or show fear or apprehension
lonely; empty; abandoned	

1. Still the lone one and **desolate** waits for his Maker's ruth— (l. 1)
2. O, well he remembers the hall-men, the treasure **bestowed** in the hall (l. 27)
3. And he sees the dreary rime, and the snow **commingled** with hail. (l. 36)
4. Full patient the **sage** must be, and he that would counsel teach— (l. 51)
5. The **prudent** must understand how terror and awe shall be (l. 57)
6. The wine-halls crumble, **bereft** of joy the warriors lie (l. 61)
7. The flowers of the **doughty** fallen, the proud ones fair to the eye. (l. 62)
8. Stood empty and lorn of the burst of the mighty revelers' **mirth**. (l. 68)
9. The terrible storm that **fetters** the earth, the winter-bale (l. 82)
10. When the shadow of night falls **wan**, and wild is the rush of the hail (l. 83)
11. The cruel rush from the north, which maketh men to **quail**. (l. 84)

Read "The Wanderer," marking the text in key places according to the method taught in "How to Mark a Book."

COMPREHENSION QUESTIONS

1. In what Old English text is "The Wanderer" preserved?
2. "The Wanderer" is a lyrical expression of a ________________ who has lost his lord, his kinsmen, and his friends in a ______.
3. What meant everything to a Germanic tribesman?
4. The poem has a spirit of ____________, characteristic of the Germanic mind.
5. "The Wanderer" shows the same compound of _____ and ______ habits of thought that appears in *Beowulf*.
6. The continuity of thought in the poem is not logical, but rather characteristic of ______.

7. Who are the two main **speakers** in the poem? From what **point of view** does each speaker write?

8. *Careworn and sad of heart, on the watery ways must he*
Plow with the hand-grasped oar – how long? – the rime-cold sea (ll. 3-4)

   Identify the **kenning** in the above lines.

9. Identify the use of **apostrophe** in the beginning section of the poem. What **metaphor** is used in conjunction with the apostrophe?

10. What comprises the wanderer's thoughts in the beginning section?

11. *I must bind my heart in fetters, for long, ah! long ago,*
The earth's cold darkness covered my giver of gold brought low (ll. 17-18)

    What **kenning** does the wanderer use to describe the lord of his tribe?

12. Where did the wanderer wander after his lord was covered in the "*earth's cold darkness*"? And what was the purpose for his wandering? Include a line from the poem in your answer.

13. Describe some of the **imagery** that the wanderer sees when he awakes from his dream. How does what he sees make him feel?

14. Describe some of the **imagery** that stands out to you in lines 57-68.

15. Do you think the wanderer's personal experiences influenced his brooding thoughts about the fate of the world? Explain.

LOGIC | Dialectic

Reason with the facts, elements, and features of the poem; sort, arrange, compare, and connect ideas – and begin to uncover and determine the Central One Idea.

SOCRATIC DISCUSSION QUESTIONS

May be verbally discussed or answered in written form in your Literature Notebook.

1. Read lines 10-14. **Summarize** these lines. How are they an example of "self-reliant pagan stoicism"?
2. a) Describe the **characteristics** of a sage as presented in l. 49ff.
   b) These lines present a kind of **homily**, a passage that offers general instruction about moral conduct. Do you agree with the wanderer's homily in these lines about what it means to be wise? Why or why not?
3. a) What is it that the "prudent must understand" in lines 57-68? **Summarize** these lines.
   b) Do you agree or disagree? Why or why not?
4. Read lines 72-76. How do the use of **anaphora** and **rhetorical questions** contribute to the overall **theme** of these lines?
5. What is the primary **imagery** used at the end of the poem, and how does that **imagery** contribute to the expression of the Central One Idea? Include a line from this section of the poem in your answer.

RHETORIC | Expression

Express in your own words the Central One Idea with supporting points.

RHETORICAL EXPRESSION

To be answered in your Literature Notebook in preparation for your essay.

1. In 2-3 sentences, **summarize** the poem.
2. Write the **Central One Idea** of the poem in a precise, eloquent sentence.
3. List two or three points that **support** your determination of the Central One Idea.

◈ **Central Quote:** *Choose a line or two from anywhere in the poem that you think best embodies the Central One Idea. With good penmanship, write it in your Literature Notebook.*

❶ **Write the Central One Idea as expressed by the teacher.**

WRITING OPTION

Do you think dwelling on the painful, melancholic (and incomprehensible) aspect of life will provide wisdom and a healthy perspective on life? Or do you think it might be harmful, or not a wise way to approach life? Develop a clear thesis that presents your point of view and support it with a well-reasoned argument. Though most of the essay will be your own ideas and supporting arguments, make some effort to reference "The Wanderer" in your essay. For example, you may find that the wanderer and his brooding, melancholic thoughts work well as an analogy or example in your argument (or part of your argument)—whether you are for or against such thoughts. You may find it useful to quote a line from the poem in your essay—one time or even a few times.

Riddles

PRE-GRAMMAR | Preparation

Prepare to think about the poem and its Central One Idea by drawing upon your prior knowledge, experience, or interests.

1. Riddles have amused people across eras and cultures. Perhaps all humans have at some time encountered a riddle from somebody in their family or community. Try your hand at developing a riddle. Think of an object or idea that you would like the riddle to be about. The object or idea will of course be the answer to the riddle. Then write a short poem or paragraph describing the object in ambiguous and creative ways—without revealing what it is. An important strategy will be to have the object or idea speak in first person (*I, my,* etc.)—like it is telling information about itself. After you have written your riddle, share it in pairs or in a group to see if you can answer each other's riddles.

GRAMMAR | Presentation

Discover essential facts, elements, and features of the poem through the Reading Notes, Words to Be Defined, and Comprehension Questions.

READING NOTES

1. **welkin** (1.5) - the sky or heaven
2. **raiment** (1.8) - clothing
3. **courtier** (2.2) - one who attends a royal court as a companion or advisor to the king or queen
4. **filigree** (2.3) - ornamental work of fine (usually gold or silver) wire formed into a delicate tracery
5. **courser** (2.6) - a swift horse
6. **perforce** (2.12) - by force; necessarily
7. **whilom** (2.18) - formerly; in the past

8. **draught** (3.13) – pronounced "draft"; a quantity of a liquid
9. **pumice** (4.6) – a light, porous volcanic rock; often used as an abrasive
10. **tinctured** (4.10) – stained or tinted with color
11. **cask** (5.6) – a large barrel-like container
12. **churl** (5.7) – fellow; peasant
13. **reft** (5.13) – robbed
14. **scansion** – the scanning of a line of poetry to mark its stresses and meter
15. **enjambment** – in poetry, the continuation of a sentence without pause beyond the end of a line, couplet, or stanza

WORDS TO BE DEFINED

Definitions Bank

- attractive and beautiful through being richly colorful
- attractive; agreeable; becoming
- easily bent
- enhanced or improved; polished
- marked with spots or rounded patches
- showing or having skill
- to stay longer than intended; to delay leaving

1. Or **tarry** 'neath the banks, or stir the shallows; (1.2)
2. In **comely** guise upon the wall I hang (2.14)
3. Then, **dappled** with gold, I must inspire the wind (2.17)
4. The venomous sting, with **dexterous** speed I send (3.4)
5. Lets loose my **pliant** limbs, in agony (3.7)
6. Across my **burnished** surface, scattering (4.8)
7. With scarlet dyes **resplendent**, lo! in me (4.14)

Read each riddle, marking the text in key places according to the method taught in "How to Mark a Book."

COMPREHENSION QUESTIONS

1. The riddles were probably put into their original form in the golden era of Old English literature—which was when?
2. Why was the riddle or enigma so popular with the Anglo-Saxons?
3. The riddles of the Exeter Book were not composed by a single author, but by many different kinds of Anglo-Saxon people. What is the effect of this diversified authorship?
4. Do the riddles have titles in the original manuscripts?
5. The riddle describes its subject accurately, but ____. It has a direct connotation with the ____ that gives the style of Old English poetry its characteristic flavor.
6. In Riddle 1, write one of the two lines that contains the most **alliteration**.
7. What do you think is the answer to Riddle 1? If you do not know, use your best guess!
8. Read stanza 2, lines 5-9. Conduct a **scansion** of these lines from Riddle 2. What is the **rhythm** and **meter** of these lines? Begin by counting the number of beats (syllables) per line.
   - **a.** anapestic tetrameter
   - **b.** dactylic hexameter
   - **c.** iambic pentameter
   - **d.** trochaic dimeter
9. What do you think is the answer to Riddle 2? If you do not know, use your best guess!
10. In Riddle 3, identify an instance of **enjambment**, and copy the lines below.
11. What do you think is the answer to Riddle 3? If you do not know, use your best guess!
12. What do you think is the answer to Riddle 4? If you do not know, use your best guess!
13. What do you think is the answer to Riddle 5? If you do not know, use your best guess!
14. In Riddle 6, identify a **kenning** and write it below.
15. What do you think is the answer to Riddle 6? If you do not know, use your best guess!

LOGIC | Dialectic

Reason with the facts, elements, and features of the poem; sort, arrange, compare, and connect ideas – and begin to uncover and determine the Central One Idea.

SOCRATIC DISCUSSION QUESTIONS

May be verbally discussed or answered in written form in your Literature Notebook.

1. What **imagery** stands out to you most in Riddle 1? Copy the line(s) with the **imagery** of your choice, and underline two **descriptive adjectives** and one **strong verb** (or one adjective and two verbs) that helped create the vivid **imagery**.
2. In Riddle 2, what lines carry the **image** of the mead-hall that you learned in "The Wanderer"?
3. Identify two **metaphors** in Riddle 3 and write them below.
4. In Riddle 4, what line or lines do you think are the most important for understanding what it is? Write them below.
5. Identify an instance of **figurative language** in Riddle 6.

RHETORIC | Expression

Express in your own words the Central One Idea with supporting points.

RHETORICAL EXPRESSION

To be answered in your Literature Notebook in preparation for your essay.

1. Write a few facts about Anglo-Saxon Riddles.
2. Write the **Central One Idea** of the poem in a precise, eloquent sentence.

◈ **Central Quote:** *Choose a line or two from anywhere in the poem that you think best embodies the Central One Idea. With good penmanship, write it in your Literature Notebook.*

❶ **Write the Central One Idea as expressed by the teacher.**

WRITING OPTION

Research the role of riddles in Anglo-Saxon or medieval culture. Write an informational essay that presents your research.

The Battle of Brunanburh

PRE-GRAMMAR | Preparation

Prepare to think about the poem and its Central One Idea by drawing upon your prior knowledge, experience, or interests.

1. Imagine battling it out for the survival of your people and your country. How would you try to help your people and your country? What role, position, or gift could you provide (or would like to provide) that would be of help and service to your country? Remember that a country in a battle involves the help of many, many more people than just its warriors on the front lines. From policy-makers, leaders, strategists, manufacturers of supplies and goods, to cooks, emergency medics and hospital workers, chaplains (priests and pastors), counselors, teachers and trainers, supply-chain deliverers, and many more—everybody is essential during wartime.

GRAMMAR | Presentation

Discover essential facts, elements, and features of the poem through the Reading Notes, Words to Be Defined, and Comprehension Questions.

READING NOTES

1. **Brunanburh** (Brunnanborough) – the location of the battle, believed to have been on or near the northwest coast of England
2. **earlmen** (l. 2) – noblemen
3. **linden-shields** (l. 6) – shields made of wood from linden (lime tree)
4. **Scots/Scotchmen** (l. 11, 20) – natives of Scotland, the country north of England
5. **shoal** (l. 20) – a large number of people or things

6. **Wessexmen** (l. 21) – men from Wessex, the kingdom of the West Saxons, established in the early sixth century and gradually extended by conquest to include much of southern England
7. **cutlass** (l. 24) – a short sword with a slightly curved blade
8. **Mercians** (l. 25) – men from Mercia, a kingdom in central England, established by invading Angles in the sixth century
9. **bairn**(s) (l. 43, 53) – child/children
10. **chapfallen** (l. 57) – with the lower jaw hanging due to extreme exhaustion or dejection
11. **goshawk** (l. 65) – a large short-winged hawk
12. **weald** (l. 66) – a wooded district that includes parts of Surrey, Kent, and East Sussex
13. **erst** (l. 68) – formerly; long ago
14. **eld** (l. 69) – old age; former times
15. **Welshmen** (l. 72) – men of Wales, the small country on the west side of England

WORDS TO BE DEFINED

Definitions Bank

a large number of people killed	inactive; unproductive
bright; shining	supplied with more than can be managed or is desired
confused and noisy disturbances	taken; robbed
descendants of a notable family	went quickly
happily; in a carefree manner	

1. The **scions** of Edward swept down linden-shields (l. 6)
2. Lord everlasting, **luminous** glided (l. 16)
3. War-**sated**, weary. The Wessexmen onward (l. 21)
4. With Anlaf, o'er the ocean's angry **commotions** (l. 27)
5. With a handful of henchmen **hied** to his ship's-prow (l. 35)
6. On the **fallow** flood fled for his life, then (l. 37)

7. Was of friends **fleeced**, too, on that field of destruction (l. 42)
8. The royal bairns of Edward on the red field of **carnage.** (l. 53)
9. And both brothers, then, **blithely** together soon (l. 58)

Read "The Battle of Brunanburh," marking the text in key places according to the method taught in "How to Mark a Book."

COMPREHENSION QUESTIONS

1. What genre or kind of poem is "The Battle of Brunanburh"?
2. The poem celebrates the victory of ____, grandson of ____, against a coalition of ____, who were trying to stop the spread of ____ domination.
3. What was the result of the battle?
4. Where is the location of the battle believed to have taken place?
5. The poem is noteworthy as a late tenth-century imitation of what?
6. It contains many phrases, formulas, and tricks of style of the older ____, but its vividness suggests that it was composed by whom?
7. In the opening lines, what did Edmund and Athelstan earn in the battle that reveals one of the chief values of Anglo-Saxon tribal culture?
8. What does the poet announce as their primary reason or purpose for fighting?
9. The poem features several lines that contain **alliteration**, a hallmark of Anglo-Saxon poetry. Copy two lines of striking alliteration in lines 1-20.
10. Lines 13-17 feature an **extended metaphor** for what?
11. Identify four weapons used by the Anglo-Saxons to defeat their enemies.
12. What happened to the Norse leader? Include a line or two from the text in your answer.
13. In the heroic poetry of the Anglo-Saxons, what three creatures are regular attendants of the battle?

LOGIC | Dialectic

Reason with the facts, elements, and features of the poem; sort, arrange, compare, and connect ideas – and begin to uncover and determine the Central One Idea.

SOCRATIC DISCUSSION QUESTIONS

May be verbally discussed or answered in written form in your Literature Notebook.

1. Explain the use of **irony** in lines 29-30.
2. Read lines 66-73.

   a) **Summarize** these lines.
   b) How does the poet draw upon history in these lines?
   c) What important vision or purpose does the poet declare was achieved by this battle?

RHETORIC | Expression

Express in your own words the Central One Idea with supporting points.

RHETORICAL EXPRESSION

To be answered in your Literature Notebook in preparation for your essay.

1. In 2-3 sentences, **summarize** the poem.
2. Write the **Central One Idea** of the poem in a precise, eloquent sentence.
3. List two or three points that **support** your determination of the Central One Idea.

◈ **Central Quote:** *Choose a line or two from anywhere in the poem that you think best embodies the Central One Idea. With good penmanship, write it in your Literature Notebook.*

❶ **Write the Central One Idea as expressed by the teacher.**

WRITING OPTION

Write an essay analyzing the use of **imagery** in "The Battle of Brunanburh." How does the use of **visual and sound imagery** contribute to the effect of the poem as a whole?

from *Andreas: A Legend of St. Andrew*

PRE-GRAMMAR | Preparation

Prepare to think about the poem and its Central One Idea by drawing upon your prior knowledge, experience, or interests.

1. Imagine being on a ship, far out at sea, during a turbulent storm. What would you do to survive? Describe what you are thinking and what actions you are taking.

GRAMMAR | Presentation

Discover essential facts, elements, and features of the poem through the Reading Notes, Words to Be Defined, and Comprehension Questions.

READING NOTES

1. **Note:** "A Legend of St. Andrew" was deemed too long to be included in full in *The British Tradition I*, so we will be studying a couple sections of the poem (abridged).
2. **St. Andrew** – one of the twelve apostles of Christ
3. **Cynewulf** – a major Anglo-Saxon poet of the late eighth-ninth centuries
4. **gat** (l. 236) – archaic past tense of *get*
5. **thanes** (l. 237) – soldiers and/or landowners
6. **galley** (l. 241) – a low, flat ship with one or more sails
7. **twain** (l. 249) – archaic term for *two*
8. **whiles** (l. 442) – archaic form of *while*
9. **holy patriarchs** (l. 876) – the biblical figures regarded as fathers of the human race, especially Abraham, Isaac, and Jacob, and their forefathers
10. **martyrs** (l. 877) – those killed for their faith

WORDS TO BE DEFINED

Definitions Bank

a fire, light, or other visible object set up high	frightened
a large, densely packed group	moving in a turbulent, hectic way
courageous; determined	triumphantly rejoicing
depressingly dull and bleak	

1. **Valiant** in heart, and with him went his thanes (l. 237)
2. Brightest of **beacon(s)**, came upon her way (l. 243)
3. The **seething** of the waters—He who gives (l. 449)
4. **Affrighted** by the Terror of the Lord (l. 455)
5. In flight, **exulting** in their mighty wings (l. 863)
6. That righteous **throng** sang never-ending praise (l. 878)
7. **Drear** exile, open torment, is the lot (l. 888)

Read "A Legend of St. Andrew," marking the text in key places according to the method taught in "How to Mark a Book."

COMPREHENSION QUESTIONS

1. Whom do many scholars think may have written the "Andreas"?
2. But the evidence presented is by no means ____.
3. The ultimate source for the poem is a ____.
4. The poem narrates the adventures of ____.
5. ____, in the guise of a shipmaster, carries him to his destination.
6. Conduct a **scansion** of the first few lines. What is the **rhythm** and **meter** of the poem?
7. Identify an instance of **sound imagery** in the first six lines and quote it below.

8. What did St. Andrew see when he went down to the seashore? Provide a brief quotation.
9. Identify a couple lines of storm **imagery** that stand out to you in "A Storm at Sea," and quote them below.
10. Identify a two-word **kenning** in "A Storm at Sea."
11. List three **metaphorical** or **descriptive** names given for Christ in "Andrew Tells How Christ Stilled the Tempest."
12. List four **metaphorical** or **descriptive** names given for the sea in "Andrew Tells How Christ Stilled the Tempest."
13. Briefly **summarize** the vision of the disciples in "The Vision of Andrew's Disciples."

LOGIC | Dialectic

Reason with the facts, elements, and features of the poem; sort, arrange, compare, and connect ideas – and begin to uncover and determine the Central One Idea.

SOCRATIC DISCUSSION QUESTIONS

May be verbally discussed or answered in written form in your Literature Notebook.

1. What are the two instances of **figurative language** in lines 242-245?

   How does this use of **figurative language** in describing the **setting** contribute to the introduction of the three sailors in lines 251-253?

2. How does the use of the **simile** in lines 251-253 help describe the heroes? How does it contribute to the **imagery**?
3. How do lines 371-372 contribute to the **suspense** of the scene?
4. In "The Vision of Andrew's Disciples," what evidence can you find of syncretism – the blending of Anglo-Saxon tribal ideals with Christian theology? Include a quotation or two in your answer.

RHETORIC | Expression

Express in your own words the Central One Idea with supporting points.

RHETORICAL EXPRESSION

To be answered in your Literature Notebook in preparation for your essay.

1. Write a brief **summary** of the first section, "St. Andrew Goes Down to the Sea."
2. Write the **Central One Idea** of the third section, "Andrew Tells How Christ Stilled the Tempest," in a complete sentence.
3. List two or three points that support your determination of the Central One Idea of the third section, "Andrew Tells How Christ Stilled the Tempest."

◈ **Central Quote:** *Choose a line or two from anywhere in the poem that you think best embodies the Central One Idea. With good penmanship, write it in your Literature Notebook.*

❶ **Write the Central One Idea as expressed by the teacher.**

WRITING OPTION: Short Story or Narrative Poem

The last paragraph of the introduction to "A Legend of St. Andrew" says, "The poem narrates the adventures of St. Andrew, who crosses the sea to the Mermedonians, a race of cannibals, in order to rescue St. Matthew, whom they are holding captive. Christ, in the guise of a young shipmaster, carries him to his destination. Matthew is set free; Andrew performs a miracle, and converts the people."

The excerpts from the full poem that are included in the anthology only relate the first part of St. Andrew's journey, leaving off with him still on the ship, crossing the sea.

Option 1: Write a 1-3 page short story that carries on with the story where the poems in the anthology leave off. Fill your story with descriptive adjectives, strong verbs, sensory details, and some dialogue.

Option 2: Write two or three more sections of the poem that carry on with the story where the poems in the anthology leave off. Use the same rhythm and meter as was used in the poems in the anthology.

THE LITERATURE OF THE PRIEST

Bede: from *Ecclesiastical History of the English Nation*

PRE-GRAMMAR | Preparation

Prepare to think about the poem and its Central One Idea by drawing upon your prior knowledge, experience, or interests.

1. Imagine immigrating to the island of England in the Old English period. Would you rather be a native Celt or Briton, a Roman (under Roman Emperor Claudius's colonization), a Scot, a Pict, an Anglo-Saxon (Germanic Invader), or a Viking invader from up North? Though you may not recognize some of these early inhabitants of Britain, pick one and imagine settling on the island 2,000-1,500 years ago. Why did you pick that nationality? What would you try to bring about in Britain in its earliest days of being settled?

GRAMMAR | Presentation

Discover essential facts, elements, and features of the poem through the Reading Notes, Words to Be Defined, and Comprehension Questions.

READING NOTES

1. **Benedict** (Intro.) – Not to be confused with the Italian hermit St. Benedict (480-550 A.D.), this Benedict of the seventh century was a Northumbrian scholar, churchman, and monk who cared for the orphan Bede.
2. **Northumbrian** (Intro.) – a person from Northumbria, an Anglo-Saxon kingdom in NE England
3. **Jarrow** (Intro.) – From the seventh century until the Viking invasions, the monastery at Jarrow was the center of Northumbrian Christian culture.

4. **Benedictine Rule** (Intro.) – St. Benedict (480-550 A.D.), the Italian hermit, established the Regula Monachorum, known as "the Rule of St. Benedict," which formed the basis of Western monasticism.
5. **prosody** (Intro.) – the study of poetry and poetics
6. **sacerdotal** (Pref.) – priestly
7. **Picts** (Bede's Description …) – the ancient people inhabiting the northern part (Scotland) of Britain in Roman times
8. **Armorica** (Bede's Description …) – an ancient region of NW France between the Seine and the Loire
9. **Saxons, Angles, and Jutes** (The Coming of …) – Collectively known as "Anglo-Saxons," these powerful nations of Germany that invaded England in the fifth century (though they were initially invited) quickly overtook the country.
10. **The siege of Mount Badon** (A Victory …) – A battle taking place sometime between 493-516 A.D. between the native Britons and the Saxon invaders, whereby the Britons, perhaps led by King Arthur, successfully defended themselves.
11. **Pope Gregory** (The Sending …) – (540-604 A.D.) Known as St. Gregory the Great; a Doctor of the Church; credited with introducing the Gregorian Chant. He sent St. Augustine to England to lead the country's conversion to Christianity.
12. **hortatory epistle** – a letter exhorting (strongly encouraging) someone to do something
13. **Bertha** (The Arrival …) – the daughter of Charibert, King of Paris, and wife of King Aethelbert, the powerful king of Kent, England
14. **St. Martin** (Augustine's Manner …) – The fourth-century French Bishop of Tours, and patron saint of France. When he gave half of his cloak to a beggar, he received a vision of Christ, after which he was baptized into the Christian faith.

WORDS TO BE DEFINED

Definitions Bank

able to be crossed at a shallow place	in accordance with; following
approval; appreciation	ordained to a sacred office; made or declared sacred
charging suddenly out of a besieged place against an enemy	persuaded
declarations emphatically urging someone to do something	points of high land that jut out into the sea
effective	to solemnly renounce
	to state or make known
	stopping; ceasing

1. which I had newly published, for you to read and give it your **approbation** (Pref.)
2. I will take care briefly to **intimate** from what authors I chiefly learned the same. (Pref.)
3. except where several **promontories** extend further in breadth (Bede's Description …)
4. the Britons began by degrees to take heart and gather strength, **sallying** out of the lurking-places (A Victory for …)
5. who had been appointed to be **consecrated** bishop in case they were received by the English (The Sending …)
6. Forasmuch as it had been better not to begin a good work than to think of **desisting** from that which has been begun (The Sending …)
7. which is about three furlongs over, and **fordable** only in two places (The Arrival …)
8. When they had sat down, **pursuant** to the king's commands (The Arrival …)
9. When the king, among the rest, **induced** by the unspotted life of these holy men and their delightful promises (Augustine's Manner …)
10. which are now preached to us, better and more **efficacious**, we immediately receive them (King Edwin …)
11. Another of the king's chief men, assenting to his prudent words and **exhortations** (King Edwin …)
12. that we instantly **abjure** and set fire to those temples and altars (King Edwin …)

Read Bede, from* Ecclesiastical History of the English Nation, *marking the text in key places according to the method taught in "How to Mark a Book."

COMPREHENSION QUESTIONS

1. Whom did Bede come into the care of who formed and shaped him in theology, scholarship, and cultural learning?
2. The monastery at Jarrow, its ___ and ___, its ___ and ___ became Bede's world.
3. Bede's education was broadly liberal. What diverse fields of study did it include?
4. Bede left a number of varied writings. List two.
5. Which writing is considered Bede's masterpiece? And why?
6. Influential though Bede was in his writings, his greatest influence was on the ___.
7. In "Bede's Description of Britain and Ireland," list five natural and geographical attributes of the island of Britain.
8. How many languages did the island contain during the time of Bede? List them.
9. Who invited the Angles, Saxons, and Jutes to Britain, and for what purpose?
10. How did the Angles, Saxons, and Jutes end up treating the native Britons? Include a quotation in your answer.
11. Who revived the Britons in battle and gave them a renewed spirit to resist the Anglo-Saxon invaders?
12. Whom did Augustine first bring his message to when he arrived in Britain? Why was he already (somewhat) aware of their religion?
13. After he believed and was baptized, what did his people (citizens) do? Did he compel them to believe?
14. What other important figure (in our abridged version of Bede's *History*) embraced Christianity?

LOGIC | Dialectic

Reason with the facts, elements, and features of the poem; sort, arrange, compare, and connect ideas – and begin to uncover and determine the Central One Idea.

SOCRATIC DISCUSSION QUESTIONS

May be verbally discussed or answered in written form in your Literature Notebook.

1. How does Bede provide credibility to his major work of historical writing? Briefly outline his sources and method for writing his history, using the information in the first half-page of the Preface. (Stop at the sentence that begins, "*But from that time till the present, what was transacted in the church of Canterbury ....*")

2. In "The Sending of Augustine," select a key sentence from Pope Gregory's advice in his **hortatory epistle** to Augustine and his monks when they were seized with fear and began to think of returning home – and write it below. Then reflect on the sentence. Why is it important in his overall message? Why did you choose it? Could it relate to you and your life in some way?

RHETORIC | Expression

Express in your own words the Central One Idea with supporting points.

RHETORICAL EXPRESSION

To be answered in your Literature Notebook in preparation for your essay.

1. Write a brief **summary** about Bede's life and contribution.
2. Write the **Central One Idea** of the poem in a precise, eloquent sentence.
3. List two or three points that **support** your determination of the Central One Idea.

◈ **Central Quote:** *Choose a line or two from anywhere in the poem that you think best embodies the Central One Idea. With good penmanship, write it in your Literature Notebook.*

❶ **Write the Central One Idea as expressed by the teacher.**

WRITING OPTION

The full version of Bede's *Ecclesiastical History of the English Nation* contains many chapters, only a few of which are included in *The British Tradition I*. Find another chapter in the full version (which can be found in a library or online) that interests you. Write an informational essay on that particular chapter, summarizing it and stating why it is significant to the history of England or to Bede's work.

Cuthbert's Letter on the Death of Bede

PRE-GRAMMAR | Preparation

Prepare to think about the poem and its Central One Idea by drawing upon your prior knowledge, experience, or interests.

1. Have you ever considered writing a letter about the death of a loved one, or the death of someone you might know? Why might this be a helpful or important letter to write?

GRAMMAR | Presentation

Discover essential facts, elements, and features of the poem through the Reading Notes, Words to Be Defined, and Comprehension Questions.

READING NOTES

1. **lector** (¶1) – a reader, especially one who reads in church services
2. **fortnight** (¶1) – two weeks
3. **Lord's resurrection** (¶1) – Easter/Pascha; the special day in the calendar of the Church commemorating Christ's resurrection
4. **Lord's ascension** (¶1) – a special day in the calendar of the Church commemorating Christ's ascension into heaven
5. **Holy Writ** (¶2) – the Bible
6. **ere** (¶2) – before
7. **antiphon** (¶3) – a short sentence recited or sung before or after a psalm or canticle in the Christian liturgy
8. **wont** (¶6) – accustomed; in the habit of doing something
9. **"Gloria Patri et Filio et Spiritui Sancto"** (¶6) – Glory to the Father and to the Son and to the Holy Spirit

WORDS TO BE DEFINED

Definitions Bank

advising or urging earnestly

an official order; commission

begun; started

grieved; expressed sorrow

fear and anxiety about something that may occur

moral or intellectual improvement

1. Of good or of evil, by **mandate** of doom. (¶2)
2. And after a time he began and repeated again what he had **commenced**. (¶3)
3. and we who listened wept and **lamented** with him. (¶3)
4. And I did so with **trepidation**. (¶6)
5. He addressed one and all there present, **admonishing** them and entreating them earnestly to say prayers (¶6)
6. This and much else he said for our **edification** (¶6)

Read Cuthbert's* Letter on the Death of Bede*, marking the text in key places according to the method taught in "How to Mark a Book."

COMPREHENSION QUESTIONS

1. Why does Cuthbert have good authority to write about the death of Bede?
2. When Cuthbert introduces the purpose of his letter, what **kenning-like description** does he give to Bede?
3. In paragraph 1, Cuthbert relates some of the activities of Bede and the manner in which he lived. List three.
4. In light of the words of St. Paul, what does Bede exhort his brothers to do? What is he most concerned with at this point?
5. What is the main idea of paragraph 3?
6. What articles of value did Bede possess at his death? Whom does Bede give the credit to for his valuables?
7. What does Cuthbert believe happens to Bede after his death? Include a quotation in your answer.

LOGIC | Dialectic

Reason with the facts, elements, and features of the poem; sort, arrange, compare, and connect ideas – and begin to uncover and determine the Central One Idea.

SOCRATIC DISCUSSION QUESTIONS

May be verbally discussed or answered in written form in your Literature Notebook.

1. Was Bede's death joyful and peaceful? What stands out to you about his final hours?

RHETORIC | Expression

Express in your own words the Central One Idea with supporting points.

RHETORICAL EXPRESSION

To be answered in your Literature Notebook in preparation for your essay.

1. Write a **summary** of Bede's last hours of life.
2. Write the **Central One Idea** of the poem in a precise, eloquent sentence.
3. List two or three points that support your determination of the Central One Idea.

◈ **Central Quote:** *Choose a line or two from anywhere in the poem that you think best embodies the Central One Idea. With good penmanship, write it in your Literature Notebook.*

❶ **Write the Central One Idea as expressed by the teacher.**

WRITING OPTION

Write a 2-3 page letter telling about the death of a loved one, or the life of a loved one who has died (or a combination of both). For example, you might want to write about the life and death of your grandma or grandpa. This particular essay may be helpful in processing painful feelings, helpful in eulogizing the loved one, helpful in collating the important memories you have about him or her, or even helpful in letting go or saying goodbye (bringing closure). Share your letter with your family or someone close to the person who has died.

Caedmon's Hymn

PRE-GRAMMAR | Preparation

Prepare to think about the poem and its Central One Idea by drawing upon your prior knowledge, experience, or interests.

1. Take a few minutes to reflect on God. Who or what do you think God is in His being and essence? Can you think of three attributes of God?

GRAMMAR | Presentation

Discover essential facts, elements, and features of the poem through the Reading Notes, Words to Be Defined, and Comprehension Questions.

READING NOTES

1. **extant** (Intro.) – still in existence
2. **Hilda of Whitby** (614-680 A.D.) (Intro.) – an English abbess related to the Anglo-Saxon kings of Northumbria; founded a monastery for men and women at Whitby around 658
3. **Hebraic** (Intro.) – in this context, it means "biblical/ Judeo-Christian"
4. **sentiments** (Intro.) – opinions or feelings
5. **Hrothgar's hall** (Intro.) – King Hrothgar's hall in the Anglo-Saxon epic *Beowulf*

WORDS TO BE DEFINED

Definitions Bank

a theory of the origin of the universe	having unlimited power; all-powerful
goodwill; compassion; generosity	

1. the power, the eternity, and the **beneficence** of the Creator (Intro.)
2. The substitution of the Hebraic **cosmogony** (Intro.)
3. He, Lord everlasting, **omnipotent** God. (l. 9)

Read "Caedmon's Hymn," marking the text in key places according to the method taught in "How to Mark a Book."

COMPREHENSION QUESTIONS

1. "*Caedmon's Hymn*" is special because it forms the first piece of what?
2. Where and when did Caedmon complete most of his poetical writing?
3. What brought a profound change in the sentiments of the writers of English literature, and in the literature itself?
4. What **titles** are given for God in the first three lines of the poem?
5. What **metaphor** is given for the sky in the poem?
6. Explain the **contrast** in line 7.

LOGIC | Dialectic

Reason with the facts, elements, and features of the poem; sort, arrange, compare, and connect ideas – and begin to uncover and determine the Central One Idea.

SOCRATIC DISCUSSION QUESTIONS

May be verbally discussed or answered in written form in your Literature Notebook.

1. According to the Introduction, what is the **theme** of the poem?
2. What distinction can you discover between the **description** of God in the first line and the descriptions of God given in line 2? Why is this distinction important to discern?
3. *The world in its beauty, the earth spread beneath them* (l. 8)
   How does the second clause contribute to the first?
4. How does the last line reiterate the distinction you discussed in Question 2?

RHETORIC | Expression

Express in your own words the Central One Idea with supporting points.

RHETORICAL EXPRESSION

To be answered in your Literature Notebook in preparation for your essay.

1. In 2-3 sentences, **summarize** the poem.
2. Write the **Central One Idea** of the poem in a precise, eloquent sentence.
3. List two expressions from the poem that **support** your determination of the Central One Idea.

◈ **Central Quote:** *Choose a line or two from anywhere in the poem that you think best embodies the Central One Idea. With good penmanship, write it in your Literature Notebook.*

❶ **Write the Central One Idea as expressed by the teacher.**

WRITING OPTION

Write a short poem (about the length of "Caedmon's Hymn") honoring any one of the following: a person, an object, an activity, a historical figure, or a spiritual being such as a saint, an angel, or God.

The Dream of the Rood

PRE-GRAMMAR | Preparation

Prepare to think about the poem and its Central One Idea by drawing upon your prior knowledge, experience, or interests.

1. Try to recall a vivid dream that you had recently, or sometime in the past. What happened in the dream? Write a paragraph telling about it.

GRAMMAR | Presentation

Discover essential facts, elements, and features of the poem through the Reading Notes, Words to Be Defined, and Comprehension Questions.

READING NOTES

1. ***The Dream of the Rood*** – "The Dream of the Rood" is the earliest English dream poem and one of the finest religious poems in the English language. In the dream the poet beholds a beautiful rood (cross) upon which Christ was crucified. The rood speaks to the poet and tells him his own story and thoughts. The rood describes how it suffered the nail wounds, spear shafts, and insults along with Christ to fulfill the will of God. But once bloody and terrible, the rood is now a beautiful sign of human redemption.
2. **rood** – a cross
3. **dream vision or dream allegory** – A type of narrative poem that was especially popular in medieval literature. In a dream vision poem, the poet pictures himself falling asleep and envisioning in his dream a series of allegorical events or people. The dream vision device allowed for the more fantastical world of personifications and objects of symbolic nature characteristic of medieval allegory.

4. **Constantine** (234-337 A.D.) – The Roman emperor from 306-337, known as Constantine the Great. The first Roman emperor to be converted to Christianity—on the eve of battle he had a dream in which he saw a cross, or the Greek letters for Christ, and saw written below, "By this sign you will conquer." He had the symbol put on the shields of his warriors, and his forces won the battle. He then made Christianity the state religion in 324 and moved the capital from Rome to Byzantium, renaming it Constantinopolis. He is venerated as a saint in the Orthodox Church.
5. **Helena** (255-330 A.D.) – Roman empress and mother of Constantine the Great. She visited the Holy Land in 326 and found basilicas on the Mount of Olives and at Bethlehem. She is credited with finding the cross on which Christ was crucified.
6. **galled** (l. 15) – having sores
7. **sepulchre** (l. 83) – burial place; tomb
8. **whence** (l. 126) – from which; from where
9. **adjudge** (l. 131) – to decide or rule as a judge; to deem
10. **erewhile** (l. 173) – a while before; some time ago
11. **shift** – a major shift or change in structure, tone, or subject in a poem or novel

WORDS TO BE DEFINED

Definitions Bank

chopped or cut	reverberating
clothing; dress	not ashamed or disconcerted
enthusiastic; passionate	not discouraged by a setback
enveloped completely; hidden	radiant; shining brightly
immorality; sin	wrapped in layers

1. Stained with **iniquity**, was galled with sins. (l. 15)
2. Alter in **vesture** and in coloring (l. 26)
3. I was **hewn** down, and from my stem removed. (l. 35)

4. **Resounding** thence a voice. That wood divine (l. 31)
5. With clouds **enshrouded** its effulgent light (l. 66)
6. With clouds enshrouded its **effulgent** light (l. 66)
7. Humbly, with **ardent** zeal. They took Him then (l. 74)
8. The warriors left me standing, **swathed** in blood (l. 76)
9. Deep buried us. Yet, **undismayed**, for me (l. 95)
10. Then **unabashed** and bold can no one be (l. 133)

Read "The Dream of the Rood," marking the text in key places according to the method taught in "How to Mark a Book."

COMPREHENSION QUESTIONS

1. Who is speaking in the opening lines 1-3?
2. In the opening section, what does he see? Include in your answer a line or two from the text.
3. Who gazed on the object?
4. What important **contrast** does he make between the cross and himself? Quote the two lines for your answer.
5. What **transition word** signals a **shift** in what the poet sees? And what does he now see?
6. How does the poet feel about what he now sees? Include a line from the text in your answer.
7. What is the next major **shift** in the poem? What **literary device** that you previously encountered does this shift embody?
8. What is the **mood** after Christ dies on the cross? What words or phrases (**diction**) convey this mood? Include a few words or phrases in your answer.
9. Explain the cross's use of **simile** in lines 112-117.
10. What does the cross bid the poet to do in the final section?
11. In the last section of the poem (ll. 118-end), what lines do you think are the most central, or best encapsulate the entire section?

LOGIC | Dialectic

Reason with the facts, elements, and features of the poem; sort, arrange, compare, and connect ideas – and begin to uncover and determine the Central One Idea.

SOCRATIC DISCUSSION QUESTIONS

May be verbally discussed or answered in written form in your Literature Notebook.

1. What conflict can you discover in lines 33-41? Identify three words or phrases (**diction**) that convey the conflict.
2. What is the cross's attitude toward Christ in lines 42-56? Identify six words or phrases (**diction**) that reveal the cross's attitude.
3. Lines 57-61 suggest the union or fusion of whom? What is significant about this union? Include some words or phrases from the text in your answer.
4. In lines 72-108, what is the journey that the cross and Christ undergo? How are they similar? How does this journey culminate in something of ultimate value and significance? Include some lines of text in your answer.
5. Most scholars view the last paragraph (ll. 118-end) as an addition added to the poem by a later poet. What can you detect in this section that leads scholars to come to this conclusion?

RHETORIC | Expression

Express in your own words the Central One Idea with supporting points.

RHETORICAL EXPRESSION

To be answered in your Literature Notebook in preparation for your essay.

1. In 2-3 sentences, **summarize** the poem.
2. Write the **Central One Idea** of the poem in a precise, eloquent sentence.
3. List two or three lines (or groupings of lines) from the poem that **support** your determination of the Central One Idea.

◈ **Central Quote:** *Choose a line or two from anywhere in the poem that you think best embodies the Central One Idea. With good penmanship, write it in your Literature Notebook.*

❶ **Write the Central One Idea as expressed by the teacher.**

WRITING OPTION

Write an informational essay on the genre of dream vision (dream allegory) poems in medieval literature. Structure the essay to explain the genre, its popularity and function in medieval literature, and then examine some particular dream vision poems (or small sections of larger dream vision poems). Some examples include the first part of "The Romance of the Rose" (thirteenth century), Chaucer's "The Book of the Duchess"; the "Pearl" poem (by the poet who wrote *Sir Gawaine and the Green Knight*); Dunbar's "The Thrissill and the Rois" and "The Golden Targe"; and Bunyan's *The Pilgrim's Progress.*

From the NORMAN CONQUEST to the ACCESSION OF THE TUDORS

1066-1485 A.D.

Introduction

Read the Introduction "Knight, Priest, & Commoner" in **The British Tradition I**, *marking the text as you read, according to the method taught in "How to Mark a Book."*

COMPREHENSION QUESTIONS

1. When he defeated his English rival ____ at the Battle of ____ (____), he became not only ____, but ____, King of ____.
2. With ruthless force, he imposed upon the land his ____, ____, and ____.
3. With the Norman Conquest, what two languages were forced upon the intellectual and aristocratic landscape of England until about 1400?
4. Crude as daily life was in the Middle Ages, the Norman Conquest nevertheless brought manifest improvement in ____, and a growth and organization of ____, an increased stability in the administration of ____, and a ____ acquisitiveness that went to make life far more complete during the Middle Ages than it had been under the rule of the Anglo-Saxon kings.
5. Define feudalism or the "feudal system" in one sentence.
6. What was the greatest of all institutions in the Middle Ages?
7. Beneath this weighty and massive superstructure of ____ and ____ labored the man of the people.
8. But gradually ____ and ____crept into the prevailing agricultural scene; ____ of all sorts appeared to meet the needs of the more complex society. More and more freemen appeared; a ____ arose.
9. The ____ of 1295, in which both commons and lords were joined, heralded the ____.
10. One cannot overestimate the importance of the ____ century in the building of the modern world.
11. By 1385, the ____ began to be taught regularly in the schools in place of ____.

12. Though literature and the arts languished for nearly three-quarters of the fifteenth century, after that it entered upon the sea of the ____.

13. After the Norman Conquest, the Anglo-Saxon warrior was reborn as the ____.

14. This change is also reflected in the ____ literature of the two periods—the difference between the ____ and the medieval knight.

15. The obvious factor in this change had been the larger role that ____had come to play in both ____.

16. Perhaps the most compelling reason for the change is to be found in the revival of ____ all over Europe toward the end of eleventh century, and the consequent stimulation of the devotion to the ____ manifest in all lands.

17. Another reason for the change is the revival of ____, from which the ____ was born.

18. The grim folk-hero of Anglo-Saxon literature has been transformed. He is now the ____ and his code of conduct is known as the ____.

19. In England, the most vital and enduring romances were those of ____.

20. In the literature of the medieval church—the "moral romances"—what kind of stories were linked to the above (Question #19) romances?

21. Concerning the literature of the common people, it is not yet clear how these ballads came into being, but it is certain that they represent the ____ instinct, this time not among the aristocratic courts of chieftains or sovereigns, but among the humble ____.

22. Who are the four great writers of medieval England?

23. The old Anglo-Saxon warrior has a descendant in the ____. There is the same code of loyalty for the medieval knight as for his epic prototype, but where the epic warrior was faithful to his ____, the ____ has a threefold loyalty: to his ____.

24. Beneath all the violence and bloodshed of the Middle Ages, beneath all the pestilence and filth and ignorance and intolerance, there is still a real ____ —the ____.

25. Above all, it was humanity ____, and it has that universal appeal which ____ has for him who cares to seek it out and feel it.

THE LITERATURE OF THE MEDIEVAL CHURCH

from *A Bestiary*

PRE-GRAMMAR | Preparation

Prepare to think about the poem and its Central One Idea by drawing upon your prior knowledge, experience, or interests.

1. What is your favorite animal(s)? Why? What characteristics and behaviors of the animal(s) interest you?

GRAMMAR | Presentation

Discover essential facts, elements, and features of the poem through the Reading Notes, Words to Be Defined, and Comprehension Questions.

READING NOTES

1. ***Physiologus*** (Intro.) – an ancient text containing beast-tales
2. ***Bestiary*** (Intro.) – a medieval collection of beast-tales written about 1225
3. **euphistic** (Intro.) – an artificial, highly elaborate way of writing or speaking, popular in English prose during the Renaissance
4. **fagots** (The Phoenix) – bundles of sticks used for lighting a fire
5. **turbot** (The Whale) – a European flatfish
6. **sturgeon** (The Whale) – a very large primitive fish with bony plates on the body
7. **porpoise** (The Whale) – a small-toothed whale with a blunt rounded snout
8. **Cetus** (The Whale) – a massive whale; in Greek mythology, this whale threatened Andromeda before Perseus rescued her
9. **thither** (The Whale) – to or toward that place
10. **perchance** (The Turtle-Dove) – perhaps; by some chance

11. **haply** (The Turtle-Dove) – by chance
12. **allegory** – a form of extended metaphor in which objects and persons in a narrative, either in prose or verse, are equated with meanings that lie outside the narrative

WORDS TO BE DEFINED

Definitions Bank

a characteristic distinctive of a particular person, animal, or place

deliverance from sin and its consequences

heavily loaded

inconstancy; changeability in loyalty or affections

striking with firm blows

to succeed in persuading someone to do something

1. Another wonderful **peculiarity** of the lion (The Lion)
2. came for our **salvation** here upon earth (The Lion)
3. the bird, **laden** with spices, comes to the altar (The Phoenix)
4. and **smiting** upon the hard stone with its beak (The Phoenix)
5. Nothing in the world can **induce** her to take another mate (The Turtle-Dove)
6. I wonder at the **fickleness** of man and woman. (The Turtle-Dove)

Read the beast-tales from **A Bestiary,** *marking the text in key places according to the method taught in "How to Mark a Book."*

COMPREHENSION QUESTIONS

1. What has characterized folklore in all parts of the world as far back as there is record?
2. An episode from what great Anglo-Saxon text owes some of its details to this particular folklore?
3. Why and how did the medieval Christian churchman (cleric) make use of the beast-tales?

4. What are the lion's three peculiar characteristics?
5. How long does the Phoenix live?
6. Briefly describe the Phoenix's death and rebirth.
7. In "The Whale," why do the mariners think the whale's back is an island?
8. What, primarily, causes the whale to plunge into the sea?
9. According to the tale, what makes the turtle-dove such a special bird?

LOGIC | Dialectic

Reason with the facts, elements, and features of the poem; sort, arrange, compare, and connect ideas – and begin to uncover and determine the Central One Idea.

SOCRATIC DISCUSSION QUESTIONS

May be verbally discussed or answered in written form in your Literature Notebook.

1. What **simile** is present in "The Whale"? How does it contribute to the **imagery**?
2. What **similarity** can you discover in "The Lion" and "The Phoenix" tales?
3. "The Turtle-Dove" functions primarily as a **comparison**. Explain. Include a line from the text in your answer.

RHETORIC | Expression

Express in your own words the Central One Idea with supporting points.

RHETORICAL EXPRESSION

To be answered in your Literature Notebook in preparation for your essay.

1. Write a few facts about beast-tales.
2. Write the **Central One Idea** of the poem in a precise, eloquent sentence.
3. List two or three points that **support** your determination of the Central One Idea.

◈ **Central Quote:** *Choose a line or two from anywhere in the poem that you think best embodies the Central One Idea. With good penmanship, write it in your Literature Notebook.*

❶ **Write the Central One Idea as expressed by the teacher.**

WRITING OPTION

Choose an animal or mythological creature and write a beast-tale. Your beast-tale should be roughly the same length, manner, and style as the beast-tales you have read here. You may or may not choose to add an allegory (moral) to your beast-tale. That option is entirely up to you!

Gaudeamus Igitur

PRE-GRAMMAR | Preparation

Prepare to think about the poem and its Central One Idea by drawing upon your prior knowledge, experience, or interests.

1. Imagine a town where nobody is allowed to laugh, dance, celebrate, or have fun. Now imagine that you have the opportunity to try to change the minds of those in authority by writing a public "letter to the editor" in the local newspaper. What would you say? Write a paragraph from your "letter" below.

GRAMMAR | Presentation

Discover essential facts, elements, and features of the poem through the Reading Notes, Words to Be Defined, and Comprehension Questions.

READING NOTES

1. *Gaudeamus Igitur* - "Let us therefore rejoice."
2. **ere** (2.2) - before
3. **thereof** (2.4) - of that; of the thing just mentioned
4. **commonwealth** (5.1) - an independent country or community
5. **pule** (7.1) - whine; cry; whimper
6. **structure** - the arrangement of ideas in a poem or work of fiction

WORDS TO BE DEFINED

Definitions Bank

shortness of time	dutiful; obedient
one hostile or indifferent to art and culture	to prosper; to grow; to thrive

1. Brief is life, and **brevity** (3.1)
2. Let them ever **flourish!** (4.5)
3. Good, industrious, **duteous**! (6.5)
4. Die the starch-neck **Philistine**! (7.4)

Read "Gaudeamus Igitur," marking the text in key places according to the method taught in "How to Mark a Book."

COMPREHENSION QUESTIONS

1. Briefly **summarize** stanza 1.
2. Provide a brief **paraphrase** of stanza 2.
3. Identify the first main **shift** in the **structure** of the poem.
4. Whom does the poet extol in the second section of the poem? List four.
5. How does the speaker provide another **shift** for the **conclusion** of the poem? Explain the shift and **summarize** the conclusion.

LOGIC | Dialectic

Reason with the facts, elements, and features of the poem; sort, arrange, compare, and connect ideas – and begin to uncover and determine the Central One Idea.

SOCRATIC DISCUSSION QUESTIONS

May be verbally discussed or answered in written form in your Literature Notebook.

1. Explain the importance of lines 1-2 for the **structure** of the poem.
2. What is the relationship of lines 3-5 to lines 1-2?
3. Which line(s) do you think is the most important in stanza 3? Why?
4. Quote the line with the **simile** in stanza 3. How does it support the **main point** of the stanza?
5. Identify two instances of **anaphora** in the poem.
6. Why do you think "Gaudeamus Igitur" is such a traditional and popular academic song sung at university graduation ceremonies and academic feasts? What is the gist of the poem?

RHETORIC | Expression

Express in your own words the Central One Idea with supporting points.

RHETORICAL EXPRESSION

To be answered in your Literature Notebook in preparation for your essay.

1. Write a brief **paraphrase** (a phrase or short sentence) for each of the three main sections of "Gaudeamus Igitur."
2. Choose one of your paraphrases above that best expresses the **Central One Idea** of the poem.
3. List one point that **supports** your determination of the Central One Idea.

◈ **Central Quote:** *Choose a line or two from anywhere in the poem that you think best embodies the Central One Idea. With good penmanship, write it in your Literature Notebook.*

❶ **Write the Central One Idea as expressed by the teacher.**

WRITING OPTION

Write a spirited folk song (a kind of poem meant to be sung) that is intended to inspire people to "seize the day"! Imagine the song being sung at a wedding or a feast when the wine is flowing! Your poem/song should be about five stanzas long. Use some poetic devices, such as anaphora, repetition, rhyme, etc., to capture the spirit of a folk song that is meant to be sung.

Everyman

BASIC FEATURES & BACKGROUND

1. **Morality Plays** – *Everyman* is a morality play. The genre developed during the medieval period in Europe and featured allegorical dramas with characters who personify moral qualities or actions, such as Good-Deeds and Confession; or abstractions, such as Beauty and Death. Their purpose was didactic, that is, to teach moral lessons. Scholars date *Everyman* around the year 1485.
2. **Miracle Plays** – The miracle play, also called the saint's play, preceded the morality play and presented an account of the life, miracles, or martyrdom of a saint. They drew their basic plots from Bible stories.
3. **Mystery Plays** – The mystery play was the earliest of these three kinds of vernacular drama in medieval Europe. It dates to the thirteenth century and usually represented biblical subjects such as the Creation, Adam and Eve, and the Last Judgment.
4. **allegory** – The representation of abstract ideas or principles by characters, figures, or events in narrative, dramatic, or pictorial form.
5. **form** – Rhyming verse in irregular meter and rhyme scheme, though its rhyming couplets in four- or five-stress lines make the form close to iambic tetrameter and iambic pentameter.
6. **personification** – A figure of speech that gives human qualities to animals, inanimate objects, or ideas.
7. **prosopopoeia** – A figure of speech in which an imaginary, absent, or deceased person is represented as speaking.
8. **epigraph** – A motto, phrase, or quotation set at the beginning of a literary work (or one of its divisions) to suggest a theme.

9. **epithet** – An adjective or brief phrase used to characterize a person, place, or thing, summarizing its most essential quality. For example, Everyman, speaking about God in lines 595-597, uses a number of epithets: "O ransomer and redeemer / Of all the world, hope and conductor / Mirror of joy, and founder of mercy."
10. **apostrophe** – A figure of speech in which someone (usually absent), an abstract quality, or a non-existent personage is addressed as though present.

INTRODUCTION

Read the Introduction of **Everyman** *in* **The British Tradition I**, *marking the text as you read, according to the method taught in "How to Mark a Book."*

COMPREHENSION QUESTIONS

1. The morality plays presented ____ and ____ doctrines in dramatic form.
2. What is the approximate date range of the morality plays?
3. During these 150 years, they retained their essential ____ character and ____ purpose.
4. **Circle – True** or **False:** Over the 150 years, they gradually changed from strictly religious (medieval dramatized sermons) to more secular political and polemical topics.
5. Is *Everyman* a notable example of an early theological morality play or a later Tudor morality play?
6. What indicates the early popularity of *Everyman*?
7. *Everyman* has a close relationship to what other text?
8. Though unknown, the author of *Everyman* was most likely a ____.
9. What are the three lurking pitfalls of temptation?
10. What are listed as the foes of Everyman?
11. What, then, are the opponents to sin?

12. *Everyman* reveals the medieval interest in the débat, which is what?

Bonus Question: The writer quotes the undiscovered country "*from whose bourn no traveler returns.*" What writer and play is he referring to?

PRE-GRAMMAR | Preparation

Prepare to think about the poem and its Central One Idea by drawing upon your prior knowledge, experience, or interests.

1. Think about the relationship of material possessions (toys, electronics, etc.) to the mind and soul. How might owning a few possessions rather than many possessions affect one's spiritual life?
2. Take a minute to think about the multitude of things that we have and experience in life—material goods, friendships, faith, family, laughter, knowledge, love, successes, failures, entertainment, confession, repentance, virtues (good deeds), and vices (bad actions/sin), pleasures such as food and drink, and our relationship to God. And there are several others that could be added to this list.
3. Which things last the shortest? Which things last the longest?
4. Which of the realities above do you think last through death into eternal life?

Read the entire play through once before beginning this study. Then, re-read the lines being studied in each section as they are assigned.

Section 1: Lines 1–118

GRAMMAR | Presentation

Discover essential facts, elements, and features of the poem through the Reading Notes, Words to Be Defined, and Comprehension Questions.

READING NOTES

1. **Messenger** – the prologue speaker who announces the theme of the play
2. **Everyman** – the protagonist in the play; represents every man—in other words, all mankind
3. **Death** – a messenger of God; represents death in the world—from which no man can escape
4. **give audience** (1, 21) – give ear to; listen to
5. **by figure** (3) – in the literary form of (in this case a moral play)
6. **intent** (8) – meaning
7. **ghostly sight** (25) – spiritual insight
8. **rod** (28) – a symbol of heavenly discipline
9. **hanged between two** (31) – reference to Christ crucified between two thieves
10. **clean** (35) – thoroughly; completely
11. **seven deadly sins** (36) – also known as the capital vices or cardinal sins; the conventional opponents of the Christian virtues; they are wrath, greed, sloth, pride, lust, envy, gluttony
12. **make his mansion** (53) – dwell
13. **thereto** (54) – to that
14. **in no wise** (69) – in no way
15. **depart** (77) – divide

16. **wete** (88) – know
17. **wit** (102) – understanding
18. **book of count** (104) – all of the actions for which one will have to face judgment
19. **ado** (111) – fuss, trouble, bother
20. **make none attournay** (112) – have no attorney
21. **rest** (116) – arrest, seize

WORDS TO BE DEFINED

Definitions Bank

a call to account for one's actions

to attack on all sides; to assail

delay

grandeur; splendor

honor; respect

praiseworthy; laudable

wealth; success

to refrain from enforcing something that is due

temporary; not permanent

weighed down; burdened

offered for acceptance

1. And hear this matter with **reverence** (2)
2. How **transitory** we be all day (6)
3. Calleth Everyman to a general **reckoning** (20)
4. I perceive here in my **majesty** (22)
5. Living without dread in worldly **prosperity** (24)
6. Now in the world be made **commendable** (38)
7. I see the more that I them **forbear** (42)
8. I **proffered** the people great multitude of mercy (58)
9. They be so **cumbered** with worldly riches (60)
10. Every man will I **beset** that liveth beastly (74)
11. Without any longer **respite.** (100)

Read Section 1: Lines 1–118 of Everyman, *marking the text in key places according to the method taught in "How to Mark a Book."*

COMPREHENSION QUESTIONS

1. How does the Messenger ask the viewers to receive the play?
2. In lines 22ff, when God speaks, what is the first problem of man that He mentions?
3. What are the second and third faults of man that God mentions?
4. What **metaphor** does God use when He faults man for a fourth time?
5. Identify two more faults of man that God mentions in lines 22-35.
6. The writer of *Everyman* includes a few antitheses in God's speech. An **antithesis** is a rhetorical device that features strong parallel structure with contrasting words or ideas—such as the one Neil Armstrong used when he stepped on the moon: "*That's one small step for a man, one giant leap for mankind.*"

   Identify two antitheses in lines 22-35; write each antithesis and <u>underline</u> the contrasting words.
7. Identify the four deadly sins that God mentions in his speech. (Here only four of the seven deadly sins are mentioned.)
8. Can you name the other three deadly sins that God does not mention?
9. What does God say about the seven deadly sins in the form of an **antithesis**? Underline the contrasting words in your answer.
10. What does God say will happen to man if He leaves man alone and does not call him to a reckoning?
11. Though God intends pleasure for man and lends him his being, man is not
    - **a.** reverent
    - **b.** kind
    - **c.** thankful
    - **d.** forgiving
12. Lines 65ff. introduce death as a **personified character**. List three details of death's **personification**. Include in your answer at least one quoted line.
13. Everyman is an **allegorical character** that represents whom?

LOGIC | Dialectic

Reason with the facts, elements, and features of the poem; sort, arrange, compare, and connect ideas – and begin to uncover and determine the Central One Idea.

SOCRATIC DISCUSSION QUESTIONS

May be verbally discussed or answered in written form in your Literature Notebook.

1. The Messenger's opening remarks (1-21) are in what ways a rhetorical **exposition** (the *exposing* of the argument or main idea)?
2. Which two lines in the Messenger's opening remarks do you think best express the **Central One Idea**? Write them here.
3. What concept does the Messenger enhance through his use of a **simile** in line 18?
4. What does God so plentifully offer man? And why does man not ask of it heartily?
5. What, then, is the **purpose** of God bringing death to man?
6. Why does Everyman not see or think of Death coming?
7. What two things does Death ask of Everyman?
8. Does Death spare or respect any man? Quote a line from the text as your answer.

Section 2: Lines 463-566

GRAMMAR | Presentation

Discover essential facts, elements, and features of the poem through the Reading Notes, Words to Be Defined, and Comprehension Questions.

READING NOTES

1. **go** (483) – walk
2. **you pray of counsel** (490) – ask your advice
3. **do by me** (495) – take my advice
4. **is there anything on you fall?** (499) – has anything fallen on you?
5. **had be** (502) – had been
6. **For one letter here I can not see.** (507) – for not one letter can I see
7. **fain** (515) – gladly; happily
8. **good conceit** (544) – high favor
9. **shrift** (552) – absolution (forgiveness)
10. **penance** (558) – a punishment given to oneself or by another to show sorrow or repentance of sin
11. **voider** (558) – dispeller
12. **scourge** (561) – agent of punishment
13. **voyage** (566) – course of conduct

WORDS TO BE DEFINED

Definitions Bank

circumstances; state	punished
to increase with difficulty	to proceed toward
knowledge; perception	repentance
piercingly	self-restraint from indulging in a desire

1. For my Goods **sharply** did me tell (474)
2. Yet will I **venture** on her now. (484)
3. Look, the books of your works and deeds **eke** (503)
4. In good **condition** I am now in every thing (524)
5. But, I pray you, give me **cognition** (538)
6. Repent with hearty and full **contrition** (549)
7. Therewith shall your body **chastised** be (559)
8. With **abstinence** and perseverance in God's service (560)

Read Section 2: Lines 463–566 of* Everyman, *marking the text in key places according to the method taught in "How to Mark a Book."

COMPREHENSION QUESTIONS

1. Whom did Everyman first ask to go with him on his journey into death to face God? Identify the two.
2. When Everyman goes to his Good-Deeds to ask her to go on the journey, in what state does he find her?
3. What is it that has Good-Deeds cold and bound on the ground?
4. Though Everyman is desperate and almost without hope, whom does Good-Deeds say will be with him?
5. Where is the first place that Knowledge says Everyman must go?

6. How does Confession respond to Everyman's confession? Quote a line or two from the text in your answer.
7. What "*precious jewel*" does Confession say he will give Everyman?

LOGIC | Dialectic

Reason with the facts, elements, and features of the poem; sort, arrange, compare, and connect ideas – and begin to uncover and determine the Central One Idea.

SOCRATIC DISCUSSION QUESTIONS

May be verbally discussed or answered in written form in your Literature Notebook.

1. What does Everyman say Goods told him when he asked Goods to go with him on his journey? Quote the two lines for your answer.
2. What moral principle is conveyed by Goods' response here?
3. What moral principle is conveyed by the state or condition of Good-Deeds?
4. Explain the important relationship between knowledge and confession.
5. What **metaphoric epithet** does Knowledge say with regard to Confession when he first mentions him?
6. Where does Confession dwell?
7. What **metaphoric apostrophe** does Everyman use in referring to Confession?
8. Describe Everyman's confession. Was it thorough and grave? Quote a few lines from the text in your answer.
9. Identify a couple of things penance will provide for Everyman.

Section 3: Lines 619–633; 654-669

GRAMMAR | Presentation

Discover essential facts, elements, and features of the poem through the Reading Notes, Words to Be Defined, and Comprehension Questions.

READING NOTES

1. **in every stound** (633) – on every occasion or time of need
2. **Discretion** (660) – a personified character that represents the human faculty of deciding responsibly; in other words, the ability to decide what should be done in a particular situation
3. **hight** (660) – are called; are named
4. **Five-Wits** (663) – In classical and medieval thought, the five "inward wits" were reason, imagination, fantasy (creative imagination), estimation (instinct), and memory. These represent the inner self, the spiritual self, that can practice virtue or vice.
5. **incontinent** (667) – immediately

WORDS TO BE DEFINED

Definitions Bank	
to stay; to remain	two
to or toward this place	

1. Therefore I will **bide** by thee in every stound (633)
2. Now, friends, let us not part in **twain** (655)
3. How shall I get them **hither**? (665)

Read Section 3: Lines 619–633 & 654-669 of **Everyman,** ***marking the text in key places according to the method taught in "How to Mark a Book."***

COMPREHENSION QUESTIONS

1. Because of Everyman's confession and penance, who is now able to go with him on his journey?
2. Describe how Good-Deeds is **personified** (his mood and attitude) in lines 619-633.
3. Whom does Good-Deeds suggest Everyman call to go along with him on the journey? List all four.

LOGIC | Dialectic

Reason with the facts, elements, and features of the poem; sort, arrange, compare, and connect ideas – and begin to uncover and determine the Central One Idea.

SOCRATIC DISCUSSION QUESTIONS

May be verbally discussed or answered in written form in your Literature Notebook.

1. Read lines 619-620. Why do you think Good-Deeds can now walk and go? What was weighing him down?
2. How do you think these four characters will fare on Everyman's journey? Do you think they will stay with him through his death? Provide a brief assessment of each character.

Section 4: Lines 772–921

GRAMMAR | Presentation

Discover essential facts, elements, and features of the poem through the Reading Notes, Words to Be Defined, and Comprehension Questions.

READING NOTES

1. By the last section, Everyman has received the **sacrament of confession** and **penance**, as well as the **sacrament of extreme unction**—to help him prepare for his journey unto death.
2. **Now Jesu be our alder speed.** (772) – Now may Jesus give you all prosperity.
3. **extreme unction** (774) – sacrament of the anointing of the sick, administered to the dying or those gravely ill
4. **rod** (778) – cross, or rood
5. **I am deaf** (803) – I will not listen to you
6. **rood of grace** (812) – holy cross
7. **brast** (814) – burst
8. **gramercy** (861) – thanks; from the French *grand-merci*
9. **minish** (878) – diminish; lessen
10. ***In manus tuas commendo spiritum meum*** (886-887) – "Into thy hands I commend my spirit" (Luke 23:46)
11. **elect** (894) – chosen
12. **Doctor** (902) – teacher
13. **take it of worth** (903) – accept it as of great value
14. **and** (908) – if
15. ***ite maledicti in ignem aeternum*** (915) – "depart (from me), ye cursed, into everlasting fire" (Matthew 25:41)

WORDS TO BE DEFINED

Definitions Bank	
to abandon; to leave entirely	to go quickly
in a manner deserving or causing feelings of sympathy	waited; remained

1. I thank God that ye have **tarried** so long. (777)
2. Everyman, I will thee also **forsake** and deny (808)
3. I will **hie** me from thee fast (813)
4. Look in my grave once **piteously**. (838)

Read Section 4: Lines 772-921 of* Everyman*, marking the text in key places according to the method taught in "How to Mark a Book."

COMPREHENSION QUESTIONS

1. How does Beauty respond when Everyman says, "*into this cave must I creep / And turn to the earth and there to sleep*"? Quote Beauty in your answer.
2. Who else forsakes Everyman?
3. Who does not forsake Everyman?
4. What **sound imagery** do you hear in this section?
5. The play opens with a **prologue** delivered by a messenger, and the play closes with an **epilogue** delivered by a doctor (teacher). Why do you think the prologue features a messenger and the epilogue features a doctor (teacher)? Briefly comment on each.

LOGIC | Dialectic

Reason with the facts, elements, and features of the poem; sort, arrange, compare, and connect ideas – and begin to uncover and determine the Central One Idea.

SOCRATIC DISCUSSION QUESTIONS

May be verbally discussed or answered in written form in your Literature Notebook.

1. Why do you suppose those particular characters forsake Everyman yet one of them does not? What distinction do you see between them?
2. Is the **Central One Idea** of *Everyman* expressed in the prologue and reiterated in the doctor's epilogue? What, then, is the central message of the doctor in the closing lines? **Summarize** his message in your own words.
3. How does the author of the Introduction express what he feels is the **Central One Idea**?

RHETORIC | Expression

Express in your own words the Central One Idea with supporting points.

RHETORICAL EXPRESSION

To be answered in your Literature Notebook in preparation for your essay.

1. In 2-3 sentences, **summarize** the poem.
2. Write the **Central One Idea** of the poem in a precise, eloquent sentence.
3. List two or three points that **support** your determination of the Central One Idea.

◈ **Central Quote:** *Choose a line or two from anywhere in the poem that you think best embodies the Central One Idea. With good penmanship, write it in your Literature Notebook.*

❶ **Write the Central One Idea as expressed by the teacher.**

WRITING OPTION

Choose a topic below and respond with a 3-5 paragraph essay that includes an Introduction with a clear thesis; a Body with organized, logical, and specific support of the thesis; and a Conclusion with an amplification of the thesis/support.
The essay should feature appropriate tone, voice, and point of view; correct grammar, usage, and mechanics; a variety of sentence structures enhanced by subordination and parallelism; a balance of general and specific detail; and enhanced rhetorical effect through transition words, appropriate diction, strong verbs, descriptive adjectives, and other rhetorical devices.

1. David Kaula, summarizing T. S. Eliot's analysis of *Everyman*, says that "nothing in the play is extraneous to the central homiletic purpose, that all elements of style, structure, and theme are governed by the conventions of allegory."[1]

   Write an essay in which you use Kaula's quote as your thesis. The body of your essay should comprise a discussion of style, structure, **theme**, and allegory—and how they support the central homiletic message.

---

[1]. Thomas F. Van Laan, "Everyman: A Structural Analysis," PMLA 78, no. 5 (Dec., 1963), 465.

2. T. S. Eliot said of *Everyman*, "The religious and the dramatic are not merely combined, but wholly fused. Everyman is on the one hand the human soul in extremity, and on the other any man in any dangerous position from which we wonder how he is going to escape—with as keen interest as that with which we wait for the escape of the film hero, bound and helpless in a hut to which his enemies are about to set fire."[2]

   Write an essay in which you either defend or refute Eliot's claim that the religious and the dramatic are not merely combined but wholly fused. Is Everyman on the one hand a soul in extremity, and on the other a man in a dangerous position from which we wonder how he is going to escape?

3. Write an informative essay on the three sacraments in the play—confession, penance, and extreme unction. Present explanatory information on each sacrament, such as its history in the Church and its role and function in the Christian's spiritual life.

4. Write an informative essay on **one** of the sacraments in the play—either confession, repentance, or extreme unction. This essay would feature a more in-depth study and presentation of one sacrament.

---

[2]. Ibid., 645.

THE LITERATURE OF THE COMMON PEOPLE

Sir Patrick Spens

PRE-GRAMMAR | Preparation

Prepare to think about the poem and its Central One Idea by drawing upon your prior knowledge, experience, or interests.

1. Imagine receiving a request from the president (or a powerful king) to conduct an important but very dangerous journey or mission. How would you feel? How would you respond? Write a brief, imaginative scenario about what the president (or powerful king) asks you to do and your response.

GRAMMAR | Presentation

Discover essential facts, elements, and features of the poem through the Reading Notes, Words to Be Defined, and Comprehension Questions.

READING NOTES

1. **Dumferling town** (1.1) – Dunfermline, Scotland; an ancient, historical town in Scotland, and the royal capital until the seventeenth century
2. **blude-reid** (1.2) – blood red
3. **guid** (1.3) – good
4. **spak** (2.1) – spoke
5. **eldern knicht** (2.1) – elder knight
6. **braid letter** (3.1) – a letter on a broad sheet; a long letter
7. **lauch** (4.2) – laugh
8. **ee** (4.4) – eye
9. **auld** (7.2) – old
10. **laith** (8.1) – loathe

11. **weet** (8.2) – know
12. **aboon** (8.4) – above
13. **lang** (9.1; 10.1) – long
14. **Aberdour** (11.1) – a historic village on the south coast of Scotland
15. **fadom** (11.2) – fathom
16. **ballad** (also known as the **folk ballad** or **traditional ballad)** – A song, transmitted orally, that tells a story. Ballad meter features a four-line stanza with the second and fourth line that rhyme (abcb), the first and third lines having four accented syllables, and the second and fourth lines having three accented syllables.
17. **suspense** – anxiety created by the writer to make the reader wonder what will happen next
18. **rising action** – The part of a plot which complicates the action. It begins with the exciting force, gains in interest and power as the opposing individual(s) or forces come into conflict, and proceeds to the climax, or turning point.
19. **climax** – the moment of highest and greatest tension in the story
20. **conclusion** (also called **resolution** or **dénouement**) – "the untying of the knot"; the conclusion or resolution that follows the climax

WORDS TO BE DEFINED

Definitions Bank

a unit of length equal to six feet
suggests; gives evidence of
conveyed; carried; transmitted

1. which **bespeaks** a gifted minstrel author (Intro.)
2. while returning from the expedition which **conducted** Margaret ... to her husband (Intro.)
3. It's fifty fadom **(fathom)** deep (11.2)

Read "Sir Patrick Spens," marking the poem in key places according to the method taught in "How to Mark a Book."

COMPREHENSION QUESTIONS

1. What is the king's opening question? **Paraphrase** it in your own words.
2. How does the knight answer him?
3. Why did a tear blind Sir Patrick's eye? Include a line or two from the poem in your answer.
4. How does Sir Patrick respond to the king's summon?
5. What has Sir Patrick seen that he interprets as a bad omen? Provide a direct quotation for your answer.
6. What line functions as the **climax** of the poem?

LOGIC | Dialectic

Reason with the facts, elements, and features of the poem; sort, arrange, compare, and connect ideas – and begin to uncover and determine the Central One Idea.

SOCRATIC DISCUSSION QUESTIONS

May be verbally discussed or answered in written form in your Literature Notebook.

1. Do we as readers share in Sir Patrick Spens's suspense as to whether he and his men will come to a bad end?
2. Explain the **imagery** of the wives. How does it contribute to the **suspense of** the **rising action**?
3. What stanza functions as the **dénouement** of the poem? Describe the **imagery** in that stanza.
4. Do you think the king was drunk when he engendered the idea of summoning a sailor to sail his ship at such an unfavorable time? Is there any evidence in the poem for this theory?

RHETORIC | Expression

Express in your own words the Central One Idea with supporting points.

RHETORICAL EXPRESSION

To be answered in your Literature Notebook in preparation for your essay.

1. In 2-3 sentences, **summarize** the poem.
2. Write the **Central One Idea** of the poem in a precise, eloquent sentence.
3. List one or two points that **support** your determination of the Central One Idea.

◈ **Central Quote:** *Choose a line or two from anywhere in the poem that you think best embodies the Central One Idea. With good penmanship, write it in your Literature Notebook.*

❶ **Write the Central One Idea as expressed by the teacher.**

WRITING OPTION

Write an essay analyzing the use of imagery and dialogue in "Sir Patrick Spens." How does the use of imagery and dialogue contribute to the effect of the poem as a whole?

Robin Hood Ballads

PRE-GRAMMAR | Preparation

Prepare to think about the poem and its Central One Idea by drawing upon your prior knowledge, experience, or interests.

1. Do you think it is right to break the law if the law isn't a very good law? Why or why not? Do you think it is right to break the law to help people if the law is making their life painful or difficult? Why or why not?

GRAMMAR | Presentation

Discover essential facts, elements, and features of the poem through the Reading Notes, Words to Be Defined, and Comprehension Questions.

READING NOTES

1. **yeoman** (Intro.) – In Robin Hood's time, one charged with keeping the law in both forest and manor. Robin Hood is a yeoman archer. A most beneficial explanation of "yeoman" can be found here: http://robinhode.webs.com/yeomanarcher.htm.
2. **jolly brisk blade** (1.1.4) – a blade is a dashing, energetic young man
3. **espy** (1.6.4) – to glimpse; to catch sight of
4. **tunbld** (1.19.4) – tumbled
5. **prithee** (1.20.1) – pray thee; please
6. **livery** (1.26.4) – provisions of food and clothing
7. **ell** (1.31.2) – a former unit of measurement, about 45 inches
8. **christning** (christening) (1.31.4) – giving someone (or something) a name that reflects an important quality or characteristic; dedicating ceremonially
9. **ore** (1.34.2) – over

10. **gillore** (galore) (1.34.4) - in abundance
11. **Nottinghamshire** (2.1.4) - the region in the East Midlands of England made famous for its involvement with the Robin Hood legend; includes Sherwood Forest and the city of Nottingham
12. **ware** (2.2.3) - aware
13. **frisk** (2.3.3) - to playfully skip or leap
14. **roundelay** (2.3.4) - a simple song with a repeating phrase or line (a refrain)
15. **alack** (2.5.4) - an expression of regret
16. **tane** (2.10.2) - taken
17. **stint** (2.15.2) - stop
18. **finikin** (2.18.3) - dainty; precise in trifles
19. **chuse** (2.19.4) - choose
20. **quire** (2.25.1) - a medieval manuscript
21. **Please God, she will bleed me.** (3.2.4) - This is referring to the medieval practice of bloodletting. In ancient times and all through the Middle Ages, sick people would visit a doctor or healer who would "bleed" them. They believed it would help cleanse the body of ill-defined impurities and fluids (some which must have been causing the illness). They used various sharp objects such as shark's teeth, pieces of flint or shell, thorns, etc.
22. **Kirkly** (3.3.1) - Robin Hood is said to have died in Kirkleys Priory (a church and nun's cloister) in West Yorkshire.
23. **dree** (3.12.2) - endure
24. **boon** (3.13.3) - favor; request

WORDS TO BE DEFINED

Definitions Bank

a statement written in memory of one who has died	personal clothing; accessories; gear
anger	sparkling; glittering
to cause to change places with each other	strength of spirit; fortitude
	to wander; to journey

1. While thorough the forest I **rove**. (1.4.4)
2. With a passionate fury and **ire** (1.18.2)
3. And other **accoutrements** fit for a man (1.27.1)
4. My name is John Little, a man of good **mettle** (1.28.3)
5. The words we'll **transpose**, so where-ever he goes (1.33.3)
6. Did shine like **glistering** gold. (2.18.4)
7. There's nothing remains but his **epitaph** now (3.21.1)

Read the three Robin Hood ballads, marking the text in key places according to the method taught in "How to Mark a Book."

COMPREHENSION QUESTIONS

1. Identify five important **characteristics** of Robin Hood mentioned in the Introduction.
2. What is the stranger's (Little John's) reply to Robin Hood when Robin Hood says that he could send an arrow through his heart?
3. How does Robin Hood respond to the stranger's reply?
4. What are the agreed-upon rules of their fight? Include a line or two from the ballad in your answer.
5. Who wins the fight? How? Include a line or two from the ballad in your answer.
6. What two main events happen after the fight?
7. Why is Allin a Dale so sad? Quote the stanza for your answer.

8. How does Robin Hood trick the bishop of the church where the wedding is to be held?
9. *"By the faith of my body," then Robin said,*
   "This cloath doth make thee a man." (2.24.3-4)

   Summarize this statement. What does Robin Hood mean here?
10. In the first six stanzas of "Robin Hood's Death and Burial," what line has a particularly ominous or foreboding sense to it?
11. Explain the treachery of Robin Hood's cousin. What method did she use to end his life?
12. What boon does Little John request of Robin Hood, and how does Robin Hood respond? Include a line or two from the ballad in your answer.
13. What does Robin Hood propose to Little John instead?

LOGIC | Dialectic

Reason with the facts, elements, and features of the poem; sort, arrange, compare, and connect ideas – and begin to uncover and determine the Central One Idea.

SOCRATIC DISCUSSION QUESTIONS

May be verbally discussed or answered in written form in your Literature Notebook.

1. Read Part 1, stanza 37, lines 1-4. Why do you think this rustic way of life was so appealing to Robin Hood? Was he more free than the people who lived in the villages and abided by the laws of the land?
2. Read Part 2, stanza 8, lines 1-4. Do you believe it was right for Robin Hood to attempt to squeeze money out of Allin a Dale? Why or why not?
3. What contrasting perspectives on marriage lie at the heart of the **dramatic conflict** in "Robin Hood and Allin a Dale"? In your answer, include 1-3 lines from the ballad that reflect the issue of marriage. What is Robin Hood's position on marriage? What is your position? Why?

RHETORIC | Expression

Express in your own words the Central One Idea with supporting points.

RHETORICAL EXPRESSION

To be answered in your Literature Notebook in preparation for your essay.

1. Write a two-sentence **summary** of "Robin Hood and Allin a Dale."
2. Write the **Central One Idea** of "Robin Hood and Allin a Dale" in a complete sentence.
3. List two or three points that **support** your determination of the Central One Idea.

◈ **Central Quote:** *Choose a line or two from anywhere in the poem that you think best embodies the Central One Idea. With good penmanship, write it in your Literature Notebook.*

❶ **Write the Central One Idea as expressed by the teacher.**

WRITING OPTION

Write an essay in which you take a position on the issue of arranged marriage or marrying for love. Your thesis should clearly establish which perspective on marriage you believe to be better. Be sure to support your thesis with logical, clear, and well-supported arguments.

from *Le Morte d'Arthur*

PRE-GRAMMAR | Preparation

Prepare to think about the poem and its Central One Idea by drawing upon your prior knowledge, experience, or interests.

1. Imagine a dear friend or family member asks you, just as he (or she) is dying, to take an object of immeasurable value and throw it into the middle of a large, deep lake. You know that he (or she) will soon pass away, and the object could be enjoyed by you or benefit others by the sale of it. What would you do? Why?

GRAMMAR | Presentation

Discover essential facts, elements, and features of the poem through the Reading Notes, Words to Be Defined, and Comprehension Questions.

READING NOTES

1. **Medieval Romance** – contains elements such as knights, kings, honor, love, the supernatural, and battles between good and evil
2. **King Arthur** – It is not certain whether he was a real person, or simply a legend. His name has been heard since the sixth century, and by the ninth century, he had become a folk hero. In these medieval histories and romances, he is the British king-leader of the late fifth/early sixth century who defended Britain against the Saxon invaders.
3. **Sir Mordred** – a knight of the Round Table and half-brother of Sir Gawaine who rebelled against King Arthur
4. **Queen Guenever** – the wife of King Arthur
5. **Sir Gawaine** – A knight of the Round Table and nephew of King Arthur. The accidental death of Gawaine's brother by Sir Lancelot caused him to become a bitter enemy of his great friend. But at his death, he repents, forgives Lancelot, and makes amends.

6. **Sir Lancelot** – a knight of the Round Table; friend of Arthur (until, in some versions, he became a lover of Arthur's wife, Guenever)
7. **wist** (1.2) – having knowledge of something
8. **wroth** (1.2) – angry
9. **thereat** (1.2) – on account of that
10. **wit** (1.3) – know
11. **chafe** (1.3) – annoy
12. **orgulist** (1.3) – disdainful
13. **sonds** (1.4) – messages
14. **liefer** (1.4) – readily; willingly
15. **affiance** (2.2) – trust; faith
16. **bestead** (2.3) – unfavorably situated
17. **pight** (2.4) – pitched
18. **chaflet** (3.2) – scaffold; platform
19. **foining** (4.1) – thrusting with a pointed weapon
20. **lief** (5.2) – beloved
21. **deeming** (6.1) – believing
22. **tapers** (6.1) – candles
23. ***Hic jacet Arthurus, Rex quondam, Rexque futurus*** (7.1) – "Here lies Arthur, king once, and king to be."

WORDS TO BE DEFINED

Definitions Bank

fainted from extreme emotion	to put for acceptance; to offer
immeasurable; incalculable	put in the earth or tomb; buried
lifted or hauled with great effort	shows; indicates

1. As a printer, translator, and editor, Caxton did English literature an **inestimable** service. (Intro.)
2. and took Sir Gawaine in his arms, and thrice he there **swooned**. (2.2)
3. And then the king let search all the towns for his knights that were slain, and **interred** them (3.1)

4. and **proffer** you largely (3.2)
5. Sir Bedivere ofttimes **heaved** him up. (4.3)
6. and do me to wit what **betokens** that noise in the field (4.4)

Read from* Le Morte d'Arthur*, marking the text in key places according to the method taught in "How to Mark a Book."

COMPREHENSION QUESTIONS

1. When did Sir Thomas Malory complete *Le Morte d'Arthur*?
2. How did Malory develop the French versions of the Arthurian stories?
3. *Le Morte d'Arthur* dwells more fully than any other work in Middle English literature upon what?
4. In other words, it celebrates not only the glories of the ____, but also pictures the general triumph of the ____.
5. *Le Morte d'Arthur* was one of many works printed by whom?
6. What single event did more to bring the Renaissance to England than any other?
7. What crafty thing did Sir Mordred do to set himself up as king?
8. What does Guenever do to prevent Sir Mordred from marrying her?
9. Who strongly condemns Sir Mordred? What is the result of the condemnation?
10. Who is the man in the world that King Arthur loved most?
11. What three things does Sir Gawaine ask of Sir Launcelot in his letter?
12. Briefly **summarize** the two parts of King Arthur's dream.
13. What happens during the signing of the treaty (to not fight for a month)?
14. Where does Sir Bedevere go after King Arthur is taken away on the boat with the queens? What does he find there, and what does he decide to do? Include a brief quotation from the text in your answer.

LOGIC | Dialectic

Reason with the facts, elements, and features of the poem; sort, arrange, compare, and connect ideas – and begin to uncover and determine the Central One Idea.

SOCRATIC DISCUSSION QUESTIONS

May be verbally discussed or answered in written form in your Literature Notebook.

1. During the reign of Sir Mordred, what was the common people's view of Arthur? What was their view of Sir Mordred? Include a line or two from the text in your answer.
2. Read stanza 1, line 4. According to Malory, what is their "great default"?
3. Read stanza 4, line 2. What advice does Sir Lucan give to King Arthur? Should he have advised King Arthur in this way? Why or why not?
4. Read stanza 4, line 3. How did this fight turn out? Is there anything surprising or ironic about the results?
5. What happens when Sir Bedevere finally throws the sword into the lake? Describe some of the resulting **imagery** after he throws in the sword. Quote a line or two from the text in your answer.
6. What are some of the "opinions of some men of the death of King Arthur"? What do you think came of King Arthur? Why?

RHETORIC | Expression

Express in your own words the Central One Idea with supporting points.

RHETORICAL EXPRESSION

To be answered in your Literature Notebook in preparation for your essay.

1. Write a brief **summary** of the fight and death of Sir Mordred and King Arthur from Chapter 4.
2. Write the **Central One Idea** of the poem in a precise, eloquent sentence.
3. List two or three points that support your determination of the Central One Idea.

◈ **Central Quote:** *Choose a line or two from anywhere in the poem that you think best embodies the Central One Idea. With good penmanship, write it in your Literature Notebook.*

❶ **Write the Central One Idea as expressed by the teacher.**

WRITING OPTION

Write an essay identifying and explaining a medieval-romance motif in Malory's work—a motif such as knights and/or kings, honor, courtly or married love, the supernatural, battles between good and evil, vows of friendship, the moral romance, or the chivalric code.

Memorization & Recitation

INSTRUCTIONS

Select a poem (or section of a poem) from the anthology that you particularly like or feel some connection to. Follow the steps below to memorize the poem. In your Literature Notebook, practice writing the poem to help you memorize it, as the steps below explain. After you have memorized the entire poem, write your final handwritten version in your best penmanship on a new page in your Literature Notebook.

You have three choices regarding the number of lines and the letter grade:

A: 26 lines or more B: 21-25 lines C: 14-20 lines

HOW TO MEMORIZE A POEM

1. **Read the poem several times in order to understand the poem and its Central One Idea.**
   - It is much easier to memorize something you understand!
   - A poem is usually a mini-narrative—we find it easier to remember stories!
   - Read the poem both silently and aloud.
2. **Determine and know the poem's rhythm, rhyme scheme, meter, and general structure.**
   - The rhythm and sound of the poem will greatly increase your ability to remember it.
3. a. **Read the first line several times until you memorize it.** (both silently and aloud)

   b. **Read the second line a number of times until you memorize it.** (both silently and aloud)

   c. **Recite the two lines together.** (both silently and aloud)

   d. **Continue this process until you have the first four lines memorized.**

   e. **Write the lines down with good penmanship.**
4. **Repeat steps a–e for each set of four lines.**
5. **After memorizing each set of four lines, recite the previous four lines and the new four lines together.** (both silently and aloud)
6. **Continue until the entire poem is memorized.**
7. **Have your parent, sibling, or friend sit down and listen to you recite your poem!**
8. **Be sure to ask your teacher to set aside a class session for everyone to recite his or her poem!**

Master Words-to-Be-Defined List

FROM THE ANGLO-SAXON INVASION TO THE NORMAN CONQUEST

1. abjure
2. admonishing
3. Affrighted
4. approbation
5. ardent
6. beacon(s)
7. beneficence
8. bereft
9. bestowed
10. billows
11. blithely
12. burnished
13. carnage
14. comely
15. commenced
16. commingled
17. commotions
18. consecrated
19. consigned
20. cosmogony
21. dappled
22. desisting
23. desolate
24. dexterous
25. doughty
26. Drear
27. edification
28. efficacious
29. effulgent
30. enshrouded
31. exhortations
32. extol
33. exulting
34. fallow
35. fetters
36. fleeced
37. fordable
38. forebodes
39. habitations
40. harbinger
41. hewn
42. hied
43. induced
44. iniquity
45. intimate
46. lamented
47. luminous
48. mandate
49. mirth
50. omnipotent
51. pliant
52. promontories
53. prudent
54. pursuant
55. quail
56. querulous
57. Resounding
58. resplendent
59. sage
60. sallying
61. sated
62. scions
63. seething
64. swathed
65. tarry
66. throng
67. trepidation
68. trifling
69. tumultuous
70. unabashed
71. undismayed
72. Valiant
73. vesture
74. wan
75. wrench

FROM THE NORMAN CONQUEST TO THE ACCESSION OF THE TUDORS

1. abstinence
2. accoutrements
3. beset
4. bespeaks
5. betokens
6. bide
7. brevity
8. chastised
9. cognition
10. commendable
11. condition
12. conducted
13. contrition
14. cumbered
15. duteous
16. eke
17. epitaph
18. fathom
19. fickleness
20. flourish
21. forbear
22. forsake
23. glistering
24. heaved
25. hie
26. hither
27. induce
28. inestimable
29. interred
30. ire
31. laden
32. majesty
33. mettle
34. peculiarity
35. Philistine
36. piteously
37. proffer
38. prosperity
39. reckoning
40. respite
41. reverence
42. rove
43. salvation
44. sharply
45. smiting
46. swooned
47. tarried
48. transitory
49. transpose
50. twain
51. venture

Rhetoric Essay Template

I. INTRODUCTION

A. **Lead:** Grab the reader's attention with a *quote, question, startling fact or statistic, scenario, piece of dialogue,* etc.

B. **Short Summary:** In a paragraph, **summarize** the section or work.

C. **Central One Idea:** Write the Central One Idea (your thesis) in a complete sentence.

II. **SUPPORT (BODY PARAGRAPHS):** List 3 points of support, using bullet points. Each of these bullet points will become a body paragraph.

A.

B.

C.

III. **AMPLIFICATION / IMPORTANCE:** Write the last sentence or two of your conclusion, explaining why your thesis is important in a larger or more universal sense.